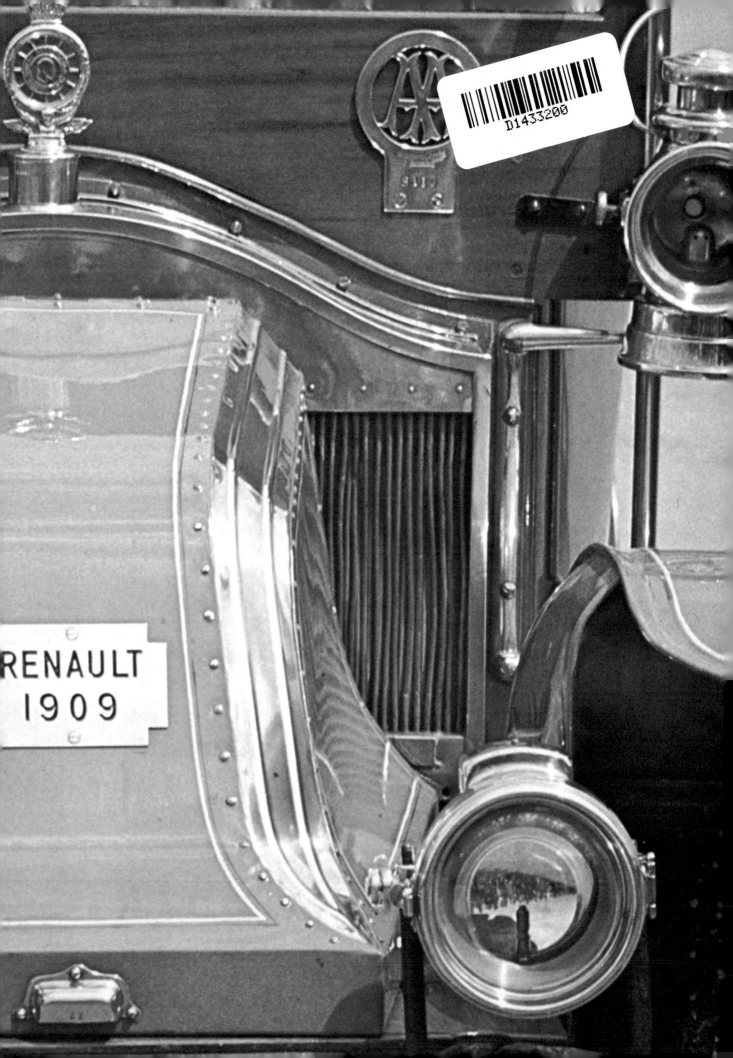

RENAULT
1909

VETERAN & VINTAGE CARS

VETERAN & VINTAGE CARS

PETER ROBERTS

Cathay Books

First published by Octopus Books Limited
This edition published by Cathay Books
59 Grosvenor Street
London W1

© 1974 Octopus Books Limited
ISBN 0 904644 22 7
Printed in Hong Kong

CONTENTS

GERMAN MIRACLE

'My heart was pounding. I turned the crank. The engine started to go "put-put" and the music of the future sounded out with regular rhythm. We both listened to it for a full hour ... the longer it played its note, the more sorrow and anxiety it conjured away from the heart. It was the truth that if sorrow had been our companion on the way over to the workshop joy walked beside us on the way back. This New Year's eve we could well dispense with the congratulations of friends and neighbours, for we had known the heartiest kind of happiness that evening in our poor little workshop, which had now become the birthplace of a new engine. ... Suddenly the bells began to ring ... not only a new year but a new era, which was to take on a new heartbeat from the all-important new instrumentality of the engine.'

Above Karl Benz; November 1844 to April 1929. 'Epoch-making inventions do not flourish in a vacuum but in their practical effect on both the individual and on the community. The inventor's task consists of consolidating various parts into a new organic whole.' (Part of a speech at the unveiling of Benz' bust at the Karlsruhe Technical College, 1935).

Top right Daimlers 'single track' machine, completed in August 1885, was the first motor bicycle the world had seen. With one cylinder and one-half horse power this machine provided the stimulus for Daimler to make his first four-wheel motor car.

Bottom right Gottlieb Daimler's first four-wheeled vehicle (1885–6) was a light carriage converted to motor propulsion—of just one horsepower.

New Year's Eve 1879. The place, Mannheim in Germany; the lyrical writer, 35-year-old Karl Benz, and the observer, his wife, Bertha.

Historians rarely accept that the motor car was invented by one man, at a single stroke or exact date and they are, of course, correct. But if one had to choose a moment when the efforts of the past were to come together to produce a single instant, a watershed of time after which it could be said that the motor age began, it could indeed be this one, tailor-made with a neatness and sense of the dramatic that would do credit to an experienced playwright. At midnight, 31 December 1879, when Benz turned the handle of his first two-stroke gas engine, he turned a page of history that ended the era of the horse. Six years later Benz had made his first working motor car, using a four-stroke engine. ...

Or perhaps another occasion could be marked as the moment that opened the doors to the development of mechanized road transport. Gottlieb Daimler, engineer, son of Johannes Däumler who ran a bakery and wine bar, had worked in his greenhouse at Cannstatt with his old friend Wilhelm Maybach for three years, developing his light, fast-running gasoline engine. He had too been working on gas engines (rather than gasoline or petrol) for his firm, Gasmotoren-Fabrik Deutz. Then in 1875 the board directed Daimler to investigate the possibility of using petroleum distillates as fuel. By 1883, some time after he had left Deutz, his first high-speed petrol engine, specifically designed to propel vehicles, was working.

There were many troubles ahead—just around the corner in fact. Air-cooling was inefficient; Daimler abandoned it and used water as a coolant. The horizontal form of the engine with an exterior flywheel was changed to an upright design, enclosed in a dust-free, oil-tight housing that contained the flywheel as well as the rest of the works. This little unit ran at between 600 and 900 revolutions a minute—considerably faster than the conventional stationary engine with its pedestrian 100–500 r.p.m. This was the engine that, two years after its performance, was to be the first vehicle-motor fuelled by petrol. Its power, one half a horse.

The First Vehicle—a Motorcycle

Daimler placed this diminutive engine in a crude wooden motorcycle which looked very like a drazin or hobby-horse of earlier times. Sited under a horse-saddle type seat, Patent No. 36423 of 29 August 1885 successfully propelled the cycle around the yard at Cannstatt. Curiously, with un-Daimler-like impracticability its inventor then tried to harness it to a sled, using a motor-wheel and front skid. It did not work.

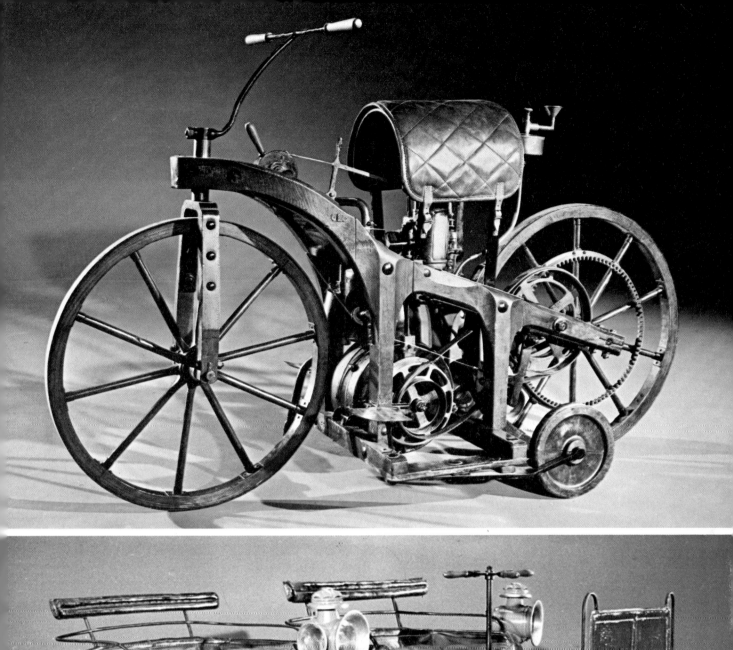

Towards the end of 1885 Gottlieb Daimler had ordered a small coach, telling the makers that it was a birthday gift for his wife, Emma, to avoid inquisitive enquiries. His second engine, of just over one horse-power, was designed to fit into the coach and to drive the rear wheels. Daimler and Maybach installed it in secret, then drove the clanking vehicle around the yard and gardens of Daimler's small greenhouse works. . . .

Thus both Benz and Daimler, living just a few miles apart in Germany, built and drove the first practical motor vehicles almost at the same instant in history. The difference in the two cars was marked. Daimler's was very definitely a carriage in which he had placed an internal combustion unit. Benz, on the other hand, had designed a new vehicle in which the engine was an organic part of the total conception of an automobile.

Daimler was elated with his initial success and, on a euphoric cloud, began designing engines for everything in sight.

Later in the year the local newspaper reported that Daimler had been seen on the Neckar River in a boat 'propelled by an unseen power up and downstream with great speed', and when asked how it worked, Daimler replied: 'Es läuft Öl-Lektrisch', punning on the words 'licked-oil' (which was half true) and the word 'electric', which was intended to confuse enquirers, all of whom would have had a general distrust of any use of highly-explosive petrol. Later engines went into a rail-car used for track maintenance, a fire-engine, and another powered a balloon-type airship for a few miles.

Karl Benz was still making three-wheelers two or three years after his first 'patent motor car', though of more reliable construction, and advertised them as 'pleasant carriages which would run on paraffin, gaso-line or naphtha' at a speed of around 10 m.p.h. After numerous discussions and arguments, culminating in giving the Minister of the Interior a demonstration ride, his cars were allowed to travel legally at this speed. Benz, too, attracted local publicity: said the *Münchner Tageblatt* on 18 September 1888, 'Without any sign of motive power, such as that generated by steam, and without the aid of any human element . . . the vehicle rolled on-wards, taking bends in its stride and avoiding all oncoming traffic and pedestrians. It was followed by a crowd of running and breathless youngsters. Those who witnessed the spectacle could scarcely believe their eyes. The surprise was as general as it was great.' The price of this car was set by Benz at 2,000 Marks, and its virtues were extolled in the automotive industry's first adver-tisement.

Right The first Benz puttered on to the public highway for the first time on 3 July 1886. Much of its construction was influenced by contemporary bicycle design.

Motoring moved to France through the efforts of Daimler and Benz in different ways. Daimler licences were granted to Emile Levassor of the firm of Panhard et Levassor, who first made stationary engines to Daimler's design, then in 1891 installed one in a carriage. P & L then granted a licence to Peugeot.

Benz had a representative in France, Emile Roger, who introduced the German cars into that country and actually manufactured some complete vehicles to the exact Benz pattern. A succinct criticism of an early Benz car is seen in a letter of 1891 from a post office official, probably in response to Benz's suggestion that the authorities use his cars for mail delivery. It is a revealing glimpse of the state of development of the automobile at that date as seen by layman:

1. The steering mechanism of your smaller three-wheeled vehicle is inside the chaise . . . in your new four-wheeled model could you not have a sort of coachman's seat up front so that the enclosed room could be all at the disposal of the passengers?
2. Could you not put under the driver's seat, or in the rear, two closeable compartments, a large one and a small one, where

letters and money for postal transfer could be safely kept?
3. *Why are there no controls for going backwards? The fact that you cannot go backwards is really something to puzzle at.*
4. *Should you not employ a more powerful engine, so that swampy sections of the road and deep snow could be easily traversed?*

The letter continues with some suggestions for improved driving over ice and steep hills and goes on: *If you are able to include these improvements in your car, indispensable for a safer and sure performance, I am positive that your ingenious and most practicable invention will be crowned with a great success . . . not only its usefulness to the postal services . . . but most excellent for a country doctor . . .*

Benz answered many of these criticisms in his next vehicle, a four-wheeled 3 h.p., 2.9-litre car which represented a leap forward in design, using a *steering mechanism for a car with steering circles set on a tangent to the wheels*, a system first designed by Georg Lanckensperger. To celebrate this victory over current steering problems (using two king-pins instead of the central fulcrum of coach systems) Benz called the model *Viktoria*. Three

years later he produced the *Velo*, a logical development of the Viktoria, and the first attempt at a small, semi-mass-produced car.

Top left Generally accepted as the world's first self-propelled vehicle, this steam-tractor was built by Frenchman Nicolas Joseph Cugnot towards the end of 1769. It was designed to haul heavy artillery.

Bottom left Gottlieb Daimler; March 1834 to March 1900. 'Success is always the surest indication of fulfilment of purpose and it represents the true value of a new invention, particularly if it becomes firmly and permanently established.' (Extract from notes made by Daimler in 1894).

Above The Benz Viktoria, 1893. The first Benz four-wheeler, the Viktoria was so called to celebrate Benz's victory over basic steering problems.

11

Enter Fräulein Jellinek

About the turn of the century a new trade name appeared on cars from the Cannstatt Daimler Motoren Gesellschaft—Mercedes. Correctly accented, Mercédès is a Spanish woman's name meaning Mercy, and was the name of the 11-year-old daughter of Daimler's friend, unofficial representative, and Germany's Consul-General in Nice, Emil Jellinek.

Jellinek had bought a 1897 Daimler and taken it to France where it had created quite a stir. Then in 1899 he entered and drove a 23 h.p. Daimler in the Nice touring competition and won first prize. Jellinek suggested that a new Daimler be built, one with a lower centre of gravity, larger wheels and higher power output. It was made by the Cannstatt works under Maybach, and Jellinek ordered 36 for sale in France. He insisted that it be called Mercedes, after his daughter, instead of the Teutonic-sounding Daimler. The car was a great

success in competition at Nice in 1901 and with the fashionable Riviera crowd. Its 5.9 litre 35 h.p. 4-cylinder engine, mechanically operated valves, light alloys used for the crankcase and other parts, honeycomb radiator, pressed steel frame, gate change and low centre of gravity immediately rendered all rivals obsolete—and it was of course, copied by other manufacturers almost before the paint dried. Sadly, the appearance of the Mercedes and its dramatic success occurred the year after Gottlieb Daimler's death.

Above left An 1892 4 h.p. two-seater Daimler in traditional setting. In this year Daimler started to use the twin-cylinder in-line engine, which eventually supplanted the V-twin unit.

Above right An ambitious vehicle by Benz, 1895; an eight-seater phaeton. The dignified company in this one includes Richard Benz (third from left) and his father Karl, in the middle of the rear seat.

Early Daimler passenger car and racing car models				Early Benz passenger car and racing car models			
Date of manufacture	*h.p.*	*Cylinders*	*Models*	*Date of manufacture*	*h.p.*	*Cylinders*	*Models*
				1886	0.8	1	3-wheeler, first 'Patent motor car'
1885	0.5	1	Motor-bicycle				
1886	1.1	1	Motor-carriage	1886/9	1.5 and 2	1	3-wheelers: 'Patent motor car'
1889	1.5	2	Wire-wheel car				
1892	2	2	Motor car	1893/4	3 and 5	1	4 wheel car, Viktoria, Vis-à-Vis
1893/9	4–6	2	Belt-driven car: Vis-à-Vis Phaeton, Viktoria, family car.	1893/6	1.5 and 4.5	1	Velo and Comfortable
1897/9	4–9	2 and 4	Car with forward mounted Phoenix engine: Charette, Phaeton, Tonneau, Break.	1894/7	5	1	Phaeton, Landau, Jagd-wagen hunt-ing car) omnibus
1899	23	4	Racing car with Phoenix engine	1897/9	5, 8, 9, 10, 12, 15.	2	Dos-à-Dos, Mylord, Break, Coupé.
1900	8	2	Paul Daimler car, 2 and 4 seater.	1899/1901	4, 5, 6, 9, 10	1 and 2	Duc, Ideal, Spider
1900/1	35	4	First Mercedes car.				

FRENCH CONNECTION

Panhard-Levassor and Peugeot, the two major companies to bring motoring to France, established it there so strongly and so early in the story of the motor car, that French is still the 'official' language of motor sport. The first stayed in the business for 78 years, and the second, as S.A. des Automobiles Peugeot, is still an important part of the French motor industry. . . .

Four years after their first vehicles had trundled out of the workshops at Mannheim and Cannstatt, both Benz and Daimler had established the production of their cars on a commercially sound basis. But whilst Daimler had been busy with stationary engines and his essays into air and water transport, Benz had got down to the stark business of marketing his vehicles—and had sold some 2,000 before the twentieth century opened.

Daimler, meanwhile, had been manufacturing his cars, but his most significant development was in the power unit. By 1889 he had built his 'wire-wheel car' and equipped it with his new 2-cylinder V engine, a $1\frac{1}{2}$ h.p. unit which gave a superior power-to-weight ratio.

René Panhard & Emile Levassor owned a wood-working company in Paris. Edouard Sarazin, a lawyer friend of Levassor, had in 1886 acquired one of the 1,900 Daimler licences to build engines. He died during the negotiations and later his widow, to whom the licence passed, married Emile Levassor.

Thus, in the hands of Levassor, the engineer of the Panhard & Levassor partnership, the V-twin Daimler engine was mounted centrally in a dos-à-dos and, as a contemporary chronicle put it: 'en 1890, la première automobile Panhard-Levassor roule', powered by a motor 'functioning by the explosion of petrol'. The midships engine did not please everyone—certainly not the apprehensive passengers—so by the following year Levassor had moved it to the front (mainly to improve steering by putting more weight on the front wheels) and thus for the first time providing a layout pattern for the future—although there is no record of his appreciation of the fact. A gearbox of the sliding gearwheel type, based on Levassor's experience of lathe belt speed-change system, was in his own words, 'rough and brutal, but it worked!'

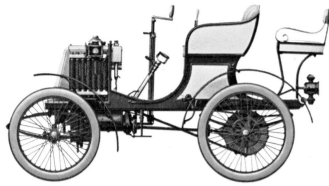

Below left The first Panhard-Levassor of 1890. The midships engine on a dos-à-dos body was not highly admired (particularly by passengers) and the following year Levassor moved the unit to the front, unwittingly providing the layout pattern for the future.

Left Renault single-cylinder voiturette, 1900.

Below A Peugeot vis-à-vis with a fringe on top, four seats, twin-cylinder horizontal motor and 8 h.p. As seen in the 1895 Paris-Bordeaux race.

"THE MOTOR CAR IS AT PRESENT ONLY IN ITS INFANCY
Daily Paper.

The Panhard et Levassor company had also at this time permitted Armand Peugeot, bicycle manufacturer of France, to build a car around their engine. Peugeot used the Daimler-patented V-twin, mounted at the rear of his handlebar-steered vehicle, using its tubular frame to circulate and cool the water. The first experimental Peugeot, modified to a vis-à-vis four-seater, made a long distance run of 680 miles from Paris to Brest and back (in the wake of a cycle race) becoming the first car to take part in a sporting event, encouraging the company to produce automobiles, and establishing the first commercial rival to Panhard and Levassor. The side-product of this rivalry was motor sport, born in France, nurtured there in its infant years, and one day to become an international sport of enormous proportions.

Concurrent with these developments were the advances being made by the Comte de Dion and his partner Georges Bouton. From steam engines designed to power toys and window displays, Bouton branched into full-size petrol engines in 1889, with a 12-cylinder rotary 'detonating motor cooled by water'. By 1895 they were selling hundreds of motor tricycles, and had made their first small voiturette driven by a single-cylinder motor of $3\frac{1}{2}$ h.p. by 1899.

France in the late Victorian age produced almost all the pioneers of motoring. The Amédée Bollée company, once bellmakers, then steam carriage manufacturers, became one of the foremost. Scion of the family, Amédée Bollée had built several steam cars, and in 1896 produced a small 6 h.p. 2-cylinder petrol-driven vehicle, from which grew a series of highly practical cars.

Other companies, some now a faded memory, some still strong in the commercial world, germinated and bloomed in the fertile ground of early motoring France. The German-sounding de Dietrich company (they bought a licence from Bollée) was in fact French and making cars in 1896, in Lorraine. In the same year Alexander Darracq, a clever operator if there ever was one, started making bicycle parts (he had sold his Gladiator bicycle factory and agreed not to compete, but not to refrain from making parts) and then turned to motorcycles, building a 5-cylinder engine into the rear wheel. After a few experimental electric cars, he launched into the light car business in 1898—and in 1900 sold 1,200 examples. The company performed a number of financial and commercial gymnastics and finally became Talbot, or Lago-Talbot, under Simca.

Chenard et Walcker was also a brisk producer at the turn of the century, also Clément-Bayard; and even

earlier, the $3\frac{1}{2}$ h.p. Decauville (a spindly light car) could be seen bouncing its way over Paris roads. Delahaye came on the motoring scene in 1894 with a Benz-like car—and lasted for 60 years. But the automotive world's casualty lists are long; for every survivor there are a hundred names that are no more. Most were built on the engineering knowledge, the aspirations and dedication of a single man, some to founder after a vehicle or two, others to branch out into complex empires that became part of the national fabric. One such man founded France's largest motoring manufacturer, young Louis Renault from Billancourt....

Left As *Punch* saw the development of the automobile at the turn of the century.

Above Two elegant young ladies in a Panhard-Levassor with the now-conventional automobile layout of front-mounted engine followed by the gearbox, and rear-wheel drive.

Below right Former bicycle-maker Alexander Darracq went into the light car business after producing motor cycles. This three-wheeler shows all three influences.

LOUIS RENAULT

He had bought an 1898 de Dion tricycle but thought it somewhat crude. So—just for amusement—he took out the engine and built a small car around it. Friends liked the look of it, with its shaft-driven, front-mounted motor, steering wheel and rear axle differential. At first, Louis Renault, 21, shortish, with a shock of dark hair and Chaplinesque moustache, proposed selling the patents he had taken out on his car to some established French motor manufacturer, but at one of the first private demonstrations, on Christmas Eve 1898, Louis received 12 orders for the model—and decided to open his own business.

The car showed good engineering. Light—it weighed only 770 lbs—it could carry two passengers at up to 30 m.p.h. and did 47 miles to the gallon; it took reasonable hills in its stride, and was considerably less noisy than most vehicles of the day. An impressive list of virtues for 1898. Within a year of this Louis Renault had made the world's first genuine saloon car; within two years he had taken part in motor racing and won several events.

In 1902, brother Marcel Renault had won the 615 mile Paris to Vienna inter-capital race in a 16 h.p. light-weight Renault, proving the future for smaller cars by arriving at the finish 45 minutes ahead of the nearest rival, a large 40 h.p. Mercedes.

By 1913 Louis Renault had built an empire at Billancourt in Paris (without borrowing a centime from the bank) and was producing 10,000 cars a year. Through his own forceful—and often intractable—personality he had built his vast works. French to his toes, Louis Renault was an individualist; keeping his finger on every pulse his character dominated the entire organization. At 36, in 1913, the back-garden tinkerer had become France's foremost motor manufacturer.

Left Dark, shortish, with a Chaplinesque moustache; Louis Renault aged 25.

Above Perpendicular elegance. A 1910 two-seater Renault.

Below Renault's first voiturette, 1899. The prototype had a steering wheel, but this $1\frac{3}{4}$ h.p. 'production' model used a tiller. De Dion engine, three speed, direct drive gearbox, and a maximum of 23 m.p.h.

19

Left Louis Renault and mechanic Szisz at the start of the disastrous 1903 Paris-Madrid race. An estimated 3 million spectators lined the route, and their ignorance of racing dangers contributed to a number of fatal accidents during the race.

Bottom left The ubiquitous Renault taxi. This one is a 1921 13·9 h.p. travelling through Paris' favourite woodland scene, the Bois de Boulogne.

Right Renault *Conduite Interieure*, 1927. Four doors, four seats, four cylinders and 6 chevaux.

Below The world's first saloon car—for driving with the top hat firmly on the head, 1899.

Renault Calendar

1898 First car made by Louis Renault at Billancourt using ¾ h.p. de Dion unit.

1899 Société Renault Frères formed. First saloon car.

1900 Renault racing victories with 499 c.c. voiturettes.

1902 Marcel Renault wins the Paris-Vienna race.

1903 Last of the inter-capital races, the Paris-Madrid, ends in disaster, and death of Marcel.

1905 First Renault taxi appears. Paris Hackney Carriage Company orders 1,500 2-cylinder 8 h.p. 'deux-pattes' taxis from Renault.

1906 Szisz wins the first French Grand Prix in a 90 h.p. Renault. First Renault bus appears in Paris. Louis made Chevalier de la Légion d'Honneur.

1907 First Renault aeroplane

1914 Six hundred Renault taxis used to rush fresh troops to the Battle of the Marne.

1918 Renault light tanks used in battle. Over 1,500 cross German lines to play decisive part in the last battles of the war.

1923 First appearance of the '45', a 45 h.p. 6-cylinder luxury car with a new line, replacing the old alligator bonnet with rear enclosed radiator.

1926 A Renault drives the length of Africa, from Oran to the Cape.

BRITAIN AWAKES

The years between 1895 and 1905 saw giant strides in automobilism in Britain—against heavy odds. As the young politician, Winston Churchill, stated in a speech in 1905: 'Five years ago a motor car was an object of derision if it stopped for one moment. Now, the horses have got used to them, the asses have got used to them, and we see them on every road'. What young Winston had obviously not seen—or he would have remarked upon the subject in terms of some asperity—were the lurking police, hidden in ditch and hedgerow, stop-watching every motorist, and delighting in fining the wrongdoer whose speed exceeded by the merest fraction that of the legal limit of 20 m.p.h. For although motoring had come to stay, a minor war had opened between the motorist and, if not the law itself, certainly the local constabularies. . . .

But then authority in the United Kingdom of Great Britain and Ireland had never favoured mechanical transport. Road transport development during the early days of steam in the 1820s and '30s had suffered at the hands of the coaching companies and the Turnpike Trustees of the country, and both rail and steam-coach enterprises were badgered and buffeted by tolls and 'arranged' difficulties in purchasing land and travel rights. In some cases tariffs for steam coaches were as much as ten times those levied on horse-drawn coaches. Then when railway companies, with the help of powerful interests who could see where the future of transport lay for the next hundred years, had overcome most of the obstacles which had impeded their progress, the Victorians took to trains for long-distance journeys, and road transport began to decline.

The 1865 'Red Flag' Act, signed by Queen Victoria, sounded the knell for the hard-hit steam coach, when it stipulated that no less than three persons should be employed to drive a mechanically propelled coach, and went on to order that 'one of such persons, while any (road) locomotive is in motion, shall precede such locomotive on foot by not less than 60 yards, and shall carry a red flag' thus diminishing the useful role of road transport to a method of locomotion at walking speed with the only advantage of conserving boot leather.

For 13 years the red flag preceded the few horseless road vehicles, and then only the red flag part of the 1865 Act was rescinded—the footman was still required to herald the vehicle. For 10 years into the motoring age, until 1896, Britain was shackled by the Act and its speed restrictions, its roads used only by horsemen, private and public coaches and the carrier's wagon. Meanwhile the Paris-Bordeaux race had taken place, Daimler had sold his first taxi, and the companies of Panhard-Levassor and Peugeot were in full production (Peugeot making their ninth series type, an *omnibus de livraison*) the Automobile Club de France had been formed, motor racing had started in the U.S.A. and Italy. And in Britain the servant still walked in front of the car.

How then was the somnolent lion prodded awake? There had been several attempts to make some sort of self-propelled vehicle in England quite early in the story of the internal combustion engine. Farmer's son Edward Butler had taken out a patent for 'the mechanical propulsion of bicycles' as early as 1884. It was a bicycle powered by a water-cooled two-stroke motor running at around 100 r.p.m. using magneto ignition and a carburation system in which drawn-in air bubbled through a petrol chamber, and if Butler had persevered, his first vehicle may well have publicly arrived ahead of Daimler and Benz. But with Britain virtually outlawing the horseless carriage, Butler delayed completing his first motor-tricycle until 1888—when he was promptly prohibited from driving it on the public highway.

James Roots made, in 1892, another light tricycle with a two-stroke engine, and a four-wheel car capable of 13 m.p.h. in 1895, and John Henry Knight drove his first car on a public road in 1896, until he was stopped, booked and fined by the Surrey County Council for travelling at 9 m.p.h. in defiance of the law which limited 'country' speeds to 4 m.p.h. and town travel to 2 m.p.h. plus the comic footman.

Little came of either Roots' or Knight's first vehicles, but Roots, particularly, had built his cars without any reference to construction techniques, and without knowledge or data relating to current internal combustion engines. Each problem was completely new. Also the motor car, to those who had heard about it, was not of great interest. Certainly, few in Britain would have forecast that it could have become an industry of any size; so those who built vehicles in the last century tended to fabricate a single one and leave it at that.

First Motor Show

However, at last the wheels of legislation began to turn due to the pressure exerted on parliament by influential progressives, and also perhaps helped along by the interest shown in a small, select motor show—held at Tunbridge Wells on 15 October 1895. The Tunbridge exhibition was, needless to say, the first such show ever held in horsebound England, and to show such vehicles, frowned upon by the horse-owning public and police alike, was courageous to say the least.

It was not a very impressive show in terms of

numbers; just six vehicles were listed in the notice, with the footnote saying that: 'every effort has been made to collect as many carriages as possible, but as the few which are in use are widely scattered, it is difficult to obtain the loan of them, but the carriages exhibited fairly illustrate the development of this means of locomotion to the present date'.

On show in this 1895 exhibition were, in the words of the programme, the following . . .

1. *CARRIAGE by Messrs Panhard and Levassor of Paris, with Daimler Petroleum Engine, shown by kind permission of the Hon. Evelyn Ellis. This carriage is one of the type of the prize winners in the Paris-Bordeaux race last year.*

2. *FIRE ENGINE for a country house, kindly lent by the Hon. Evelyn Ellis, worked by a Daimler Petroleum Engine and built by the same makers as the preceding exhibit.*
The local Volunteer Fire Brigade, under Capt. Tinne will give a Demonstration with this Engine, in which Mr. Evelyn Ellis will probably take part.

3. *TRICYCLE worked by Petroleum Motor with electric spark ignition, shown by Messrs. De Dion & Bouton of Paris, after the design of Count de Dion and M. Bouton. The weight is about 90 lbs.*

4. *STEAM HORSE, attached to a carriage, shown by Messrs. De Dion & Bouton of Paris.*

5. *TRICYCLE, exhibited by M. Guedon for the Gladiator Cycle Company of France. The horse-power is about two-thirds, the fuel is mineral naphtha, and the ignition is by the electric spark. The carbonizer, in this motor, is dispensed with. The weight is approximately 112 lbs. The pedals are used to start, but, when the motor runs, the pedals are automatically disconnected.*

6. *VIS-A-VIS built by Messrs Peugeot of Paris, fitted with a Daimler Engine, supplied by Messrs. Panhard and Levassor, and shown by Sir David Salomons. The weight of*

this carriage is 13 cwt, and is intended to run 180 to 200 miles without recharging. The horse-power is $3\frac{3}{4}$; the speed on a hill of 10 percent inclination is about four miles per hour, and on the level fifteen miles per hour, maximum.

Not much in the way of variety perhaps—only two genuine four-wheel motor cars were present—but an event which opened the doors, just a crack, to the age of motoring in England.

This was followed by London's first motor show, forerunners of three-quarters of a century of annual shows. Former cycle manufacturer, pioneer automobilist, financial juggler and entrepreneur, H. J. Lawson was wildly enthusiastic about the new motor car, and had bought up motor patents right, left and centre. He mounted his first major show in May 1896, and used his influence later in the year in an effort to pressurize parliament into removing the 4 m.p.h. speed limit which had rendered most of his patents ineffective. And when the Prince of Wales, leader of fashion and all things fashionable added his considerable weight to the cause by letting it be known that he would like to try out a motor car, it was a fair bet that many members of the House would be sympathetic to the advancement of mechanical mobility.

They were, and on 14 November 1896 members of the Motor Car Club drove their cars in a great rally from London to Brighton on the south coast to herald in the new 12 m.p.h. speed limit and the final disappearance of the footman and his (by then symbolic) red flag.

Said the year-old motor magazine *The Autocar* in terms which may now be seen as naively optimistic: 'Yesterday the proverbial blind eyes of justice refused

to see anything but an ugly, unwieldy, smoking, puffing, traction road engine when an autocar passed by, whilst today, with the bandage removed, that good lady recognizes in the same vehicle a light, handy carriage, travelling anywhere with the ease and facility of a cycle, with but little noise, no smoke and a minimum of other objectionable features'.

Even though a large proportion of the administrators of the law had been diehard horseflesh men, it did not mean that all men of substance and talent were unaware of the changing times. In addition to Lawson, who had floated the Daimler Motor Company in 1896 with Gottlieb Daimler as a director, a young engineer called

Frederick Lanchester who had given up trying to design flying machines after realizing that engine-technology was not yet ready to leave the ground, had turned his talent to motor car design. His plans were unique in that his car owed nothing to carriage design influence, nor his engine to stationary-unit tradition. Lanchester's first car of 1895 was steered by tiller—but a finely balanced system of steering and rigid tubular frame helped to give the car stability, and his 5 h.p. air-cooled single-cylinder engine had a mechanically operated inlet valve. The Lanchester was in fact England's first successful four-wheeled motor car, and in 1900 it was to become Britain's first home-designed

The 1900 Thousand Miles Trial,
Britain's first motor sport event,
introduced the public at large to the
motor car for the first time.
Here competitors assemble before the start.

production car.

Whilst the motor industry in Britain could not be said to have exploded into life after the 'Emancipation' Act of 1896, the first Daimlers trundled out of the Coventry factory in 1897, and Herbert Austin had already (in 1895) built a three-wheeler for his master, Frederick Wolseley for whom he was managing the somewhat pedestrian Wolseley Sheep Shearing Company. His first vehicle was based on the Bollée design (a sure indication of Austin's plans to build for the popular market) and the burgeoning auto industry saw him with a four-wheeled car (a Wolseley—Austin made the first car under his own name in 1906) which he presented to the Crystal Palace Exhibition in 1900.

In Coventry, Thomas Humber was turning from the popular machine of the day, the bicycle, to autocars and produced his first experimental car for exhibition right on target, in 1896, when everything was happening. However, this company was also part of the Lawson empire, and was made to produce vehicles based on Pennington principles, after the gentleman of that name from Chicago had sold his patents for a reputed £100,000 to the free-spending Harry Lawson. These designs were so unsuccessful and Pennington himself so devious in his dealings that he proved to be the reef on which the other smart operator, Lawson, foundered.

Above The Sunbeam-Mabley, 1901. This voiturette housed a De Dion motor and had its road wheels in a diamond formation, supposedly to prevent skidding. It was manufactured by John Marston Limited of Wolverhampton, formerly japanware and bicycle makers.

Top right The incredible Pennington. Its inventor sold the patents for £100,000 to Harry Lawson the British entrepreneur. The engine was a 2-cylinder 1,868 c.c. unit, bicycle saddles were the seating fore and aft, and room for four more was provided on side platforms.

Bottom right Another British oddity, the Singer Motor Wheel, with power unit built into the front wheel. The company sold tricars, derivatives of this motor tricycle, until 1907.

Twentieth Century Change

By late 1900 several manufacturers were becoming firmly established. Five years earlier the portly Prince of Wales had taken his first historic motor car ride, a journey that induced a change in the attitude of many British aristocrats towards the car, and brought new work and new skills and new hopes of a bright future to numbers of Midland workers. Daimler, Humber, Wolseley, Lanchester were making motors, newcomer Montague Napier had begun production after modifying a Panhard, and John Marston Limited of Wolverhampton was making Sunbeams (then called Sunbeam Mableys, curious diamond-shaped light cars) and a number of other companies and marques, all long since gone to their graves, were budding.

When in 1900 the great 1,000 Miles Trial—the first properly organized sporting event in Britain even though it was rather a champagne-and-sandwiches affair—took place, the motor car was at last introduced to a wide public, 90 percent of whom had never seen one before. It was an extremely ambitious sporting event by the standards of the day, and in typical late Victorian manner the organizers blithely assumed that everyone knew everyone else in a certain section of society, and the competitors (over a hundred of them) were invited to a breakfast of bacon-and-kidneys at Calcot Park, the elegant Reading home of Alfred Harmsworth.

The first day's 118 miles to Bristol was no simple jaunt for the autocarists of 1900. They were advised to order petrol from a list of suppliers in advance—mostly ironmongers or chemists—and were given a long list of repairers—blacksmiths, who else? The route then turned north from Bristol to Worcester, Birmingham, Manchester, followed by a timed hill climb on the way

to Shap Fell and Edinburgh. A swing south then took the survivors through Newcastle, Leeds, (the route was deliberately designed to exhibit the vehicles to the greatest number of spectators) Sheffield, Nottingham and London. Happily for the organizers, the Automobile Club of Great Britain and Ireland (later the R.A.C.) few competitors fell by the wayside. This tough and dusty thousand miles of motoring did encounter occasional hostility from the horse fraternity and one or two competitors were shooed out of pubs because they disturbed both horses and drinkers.

The 1,000 Miles Trial, perhaps even more than the Brighton Run of four years earlier, served to lay the foundation of the British motor industries by the interest it created. And that interest was backed up, this time, by firm orders from the more affluent section of the public.

Harry Lawson's attempt to create a motor industry with himself as its central figure produced what must have been some of the first genuine publicity campaigns to win the public away from the horse-and-carriage syndrome. One extract from the elaborate prospectus issued by the company makes its point thus: 'Horses work for a few hours only, motors keep on incessantly. Horses shy and take fright, motors cannot. Horses fall down and run lame, motors never slip anywhere. Horses eat as much resting as working, motors require nothing when at rest. Horses sicken and die, with entire loss, motors can be renewed in any part . . .' Naive it may have been, and under today's trade description regulations a plum for legal action, but it had its appeal to would-be investors who could see a decade or so ahead.

Patent-buying Lawson was seen as a towering nuisance by many in the infant motor trade in late Victorian days. His attempt to corner the motor market has been compared with Selden's early hold on the U.S. motor industry. But Harry Lawson, for all his wild and sometimes undisciplined attempts to buy himself into the monarchy of the new industry, and his subsequent failure, was gifted with an astonishing foresight. He wrote in 1896 about the future uses of the internal combustion engine: 'As we note the advance which has already been made towards greatly increased power, coupled with a minimum of weight in motor power, we shall have no difficulty in realizing that by applying these to the various forms of devices for aerial navigation, we are approaching the realization of the dream of countless generations of men, that invasion of the air around us *which will surely revolutionize the arts of war as those of peace,* in fact, the entire system of existence of this planet of ours.'

At this date, Queen Victoria still had four years of rule, the Boer War had not been fought and heavier-than-air flight was not far from the Leonardo da Vinci stage. And the number of people in Britain who had ever seen a motor car could be seated in a small coffee-house. Lawson also forecast motorways, motorcycle police, and station car-parks for commuters.

TILLERS AND SOLIDS

In the days of the central pivot, the single-king-pin system in which the directional axle swings around a central axis—as in a mid-nineteenth century coach—the tiller would have been the logical development after the reins disappeared.

Curiously, though, the first motor vehicle, designed and built by Frenchman Cugnot in 1769–71 has a skeletal form of steering wheel, and the now somewhat discredited Markus gasoline 'cart' has a diminutive but definite steering wheel. The first Benz employed a sort of tram lever, the first Daimler a type of horizontal handlebar and central pivot steering mechanism. A couple of years later they had evolved a rudimentary steering wheel (Benz) and a boat-like tiller (Daimler).

Neither of them had seemed to have heard of the coachbuilder to the Royal Court of Bavaria, one Georg

Lanckensperger, who had developed a dual king-pin system of steering, but by chance or by a little clandestine investigation, Benz brought out his Viktoria with its 'steering mechanism with steering circles set at a tangent to the wheels' in 1893 (which was not vastly different from the Lanckensperger system) thus setting the pattern for modern steering, so the history books say. However a glance at Daimler's 'wire-wheel' car of four years earlier shows a steering system operating, in principle if not in practice, in much the same way. . . .

Soon, simple ergonomics suggested that the steering wheel was the best directional control, and by 1899 almost every car (except some British ones) was steered by a wheel, at first mounted on an upright column, and later, often festooned with a number of other controls, on a raked steering column.

Road wheels took a leap forward in development the day in 1888 a Belfast schoolboy named Dunlop asked his father to help him win a tricycle race. Dad—John Boyd Dunlop—wrapped two rubber tubes around the rear wheels, pumped air into them—and the boy won.

Lightweight bicycle-spoke wheels were considered too flimsy for the first of the heavier breed of cars, which were usually fitted with 'artillery' wheels with wooden spokes and gun-carriage appearance. Solid tyres of steel were shrunk on to the rim until they were replaced by rubber, which had been used for years on cycles.

Below Artillery-type wheels were used well into the 'twenties by some manufacturers: firstly using the traditional wooden wheel of the cart, then lighter pressed-steel wheels of similar design. Here, wooden wheels for the early motor industry are being made in a small French workshop.

Cycles had also used air-filled tyres for some time, but many automobilists were reluctant to risk their horseless carriages on this dubious invention. However in 1895 the French brothers Michelin fitted pneumatic tyres to their Peugeot and entered it in the Paris–Bordeaux race. The air-filled tyres were torn to shreds by the end of the race, but the Michelins painstakingly developed their product into a worthwhile proposition. Worthwhile that was for the motorist who at the turn of the century was prepared to carry a full tool kit and to use it for one of a hundred small failures that could necessitate 'getting out and under' his temperamental vehicle. Tyre repairs were just one more familiar chore—though it meant removing the case, finding the puncture, repairing it on the spot, replacing the tube under the tyre and inflating the thing up again with a small hand pump.

Nevertheless by 1900 everyone was on pneumatic tyres—and had to buy a new set every 4,000 miles or so. Low pressure tyres were not to be introduced until over twenty years later, and tubeless more than half a century after the Michelins first fitted their Peugeot with treadless air-filled tyres.

Above *Economical, flexible, firm*, says the 1900 French advertisement. Perhaps the last was more accurate than the first two.

Below A vertical steering column with a 'two-handle' lever. Rather like a tram steering lever it could cope only with slow speed and gentle corners.

Far right Steering wheel on a raked column, circa 1905.

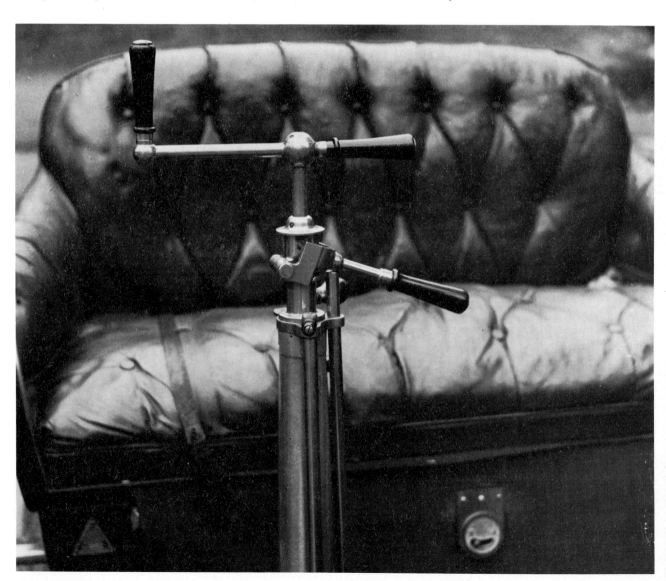

PASSENGERS OF IMPORTANCE...
AND THEIR MERCEDES

Many of Europe's royal families and top military and political brass took to the automobile early in its life, and were seen, on and off parade, in the fashionably expensive cars of the Edwardian period. Here are a few, frozen by the camera for posterity in their long-ago vehicles.

Top left Kaiser Wilhelm II enters his Mercedes 28/60 h.p. Landaulet with due ceremony.

Above Crown Prince Wilhelm of Germany takes a brace of ladies for a spin, 1905.

Below Tsar Nicholas of Russia and daughters visit the scene of Russian army manoeuvres, 1911.

AMERICA THE BRAVE

The United States was fertile soil for the development of commerce in many ways, and in no way more so than for the germination and rapid growth of a transport industry.

At the end of the Victorian century America was on the brink of its commercial explosion. Most of its industries had become established—agriculture, stock-breeding, mining, manufacturing—and the problem of moving goods from seller to buyer was becoming acute in a country whose backyard was around three million square miles in area, and whose roads were so few and so bad that many considered it easier to sail round the continent than to travel across it.

Some two thousand different makes of automobile have been registered in the United States since the first Duryea rolled out of the shed. Historic upheavals weeded out about 99 per cent of them, leaving the hardcore of manufacturers we know today, marques that have come through the melting pot of wars, changing needs and fashions, through mergers and booms and depressions.

But what of the brave new worlders of the America of the end of the last century, those garden-shed engineers who tinkered with their high-wheeled horse buggies, stripping off shafts and leather and brass and fitting in their popping little one-cylinder motors. That they built their spindly cars at the right time in history is undeniable, that they chose the internal combustion engine to propel them was, in most cases, just lucky (steam and electricity had a firm following) and that a number should win through to become genuine manufacturers was nothing less than astonishing, for the America of that day was overwhelmingly agri-cultural—farm boys were not renowned for mechanical ability, and railroad engineers were often somewhat heavyweight in design concept.

If one ignores the Selden episode—which dates from 1877 when the smart young lawyer began his long process of patenting just about everything concerned with a gasoline-engine, insisting that he had invented the motor car long before Daimler and Benz—it can be said that it all started with the brothers Duryea after their car won the 1895 Chicago Times-Herald race, the first motor sport event in the U.S.A.

This win (the only other car to finish the 54-mile road race was a Benz) attracted the attention of the country's rich, who were up to then buying European Daimlers, Panhards, De Dion-Boutons and the like for their pleasure and amusement.

Buggy and Buckboard

Charles and Frank Duryea's car was a decade behind these in development. If early motor industry in the United States was happily free of the cloying traditions of Europe, it had certainly inherited the country-crude buggy and buckboard custom. The Duryea, and most of the first models put out by contemporaries—Haynes, Olds, Ford—were based on the buggy suspension, such as it was, and the bicycle frame. But although they may not have had the sophistication of their European counterparts, these rough vehicles had one strong asset; they were made like carthorses, to do the work of carthorses as often as not, and built to withstand the tremendous pounding they would receive travelling on the muddy, rutted or corduroy (logged) roads of the day. They were built, not for idle pleasure but for the fundamental tasks of transport, conveying passengers or goods from the railroad terminals to farm or store.

As Napoleon once commented during his Polish campaign, 'Out of water, air, earth and fire, God created a fifth element—mud', and there was as much of it on American highways at the beginning of the twentieth century as there was in Poland in the early nineteenth, for even in places like Kansas City and New Orleans three-quarters of the roads were unsurfaced dirt. This and other influences dictated the design of the first cars—high ground clearance, light but strong construction, and above all simplicity of operation. A British journal mentions the appalling state of American roads in a paragraph in 1903, '"Good roads" in England and "good roads" in the United States are hardly synonymous terms,' it said. 'The average country roads in this country would be honoured by the term boule-vard in America, and the average country road in America would be called something too strong to be reproduced in print by the English automobilist.' And it took 30 years from the date of this comment for American roads to catch up. . . .

The rural doctor and the commercial traveller were the first to take advantage of the new locomotion. Then the cyclist; he had been a pioneer of mobility and the taste of freedom had whetted his appetite for more dis-tant pastures. He too wanted a self-propelled vehicle to take the kids into the country, or to travel to the next town to visit the old folks. So in the United States the car, almost from its earliest days, was made accessible to the mass of people—not just the rich as in Europe; engi-neers such as Ford and Olds showed a strong desire to give the people what they wanted and could afford.

The early one-cylinder Duryea, the Haynes (first car 1894), Ransom Old's car (seen in 1896), the first Fords, Cadillacs, Popes of various lineages, Packards, Peer-lesses, Pierces, Remingtons, some steered by tiller and braked by spoon or sprag, brought, if not total mobility,

Above '. . . easier to sail round than travel across it' said some of the American continent. This improbable-looking shot was taken in 1900 outside a *roadhouse* in Alaska!

a fair share of summer outings to a wide section of the American public. The art of driving them was soon picked up by the eager new motorist who had just moved the corn-bin out of the stable to make room for the new machine, and novice pilots would twist the crank until the one-cylinder engine coughed into wheezy life, shaking and bouncing the buggy-car like a coracle in a gale. Racing up into the driving seat before the motor sank back into silence the driver would advance the ignition, put the thing into gear and plunge bucking down the street at maybe 10 miles an hour. Advice, often coyly given in newspaper features, such as: '. . . however fond you may be of the lady, disaster will result if you endeavour to steer with one hand, and embrace your lady-love with the other. Both cars and ladies want your whole attention, and it is better to do one thing at a time', was avidly read.

Said a newspaper of 1903 helpfully to older readers: 'We must make up our minds to them and try to get used to them as quickly as we can. Their pace is, of course, a little terrifying . . . we must get over our fear; and when we have done that we shall find that our fear was responsible for nearly all the danger'. Great stuff, but not much use to the nervous owner of a new Studebaker Model C with its midships flat-twin motor, chain drive, and levers and pedals all over the place.

By 1907 many American automotive products had taken a few leaves out of European design trends. Designers had abandoned high-wheeled buggies with the engine under the seat for the Levassor system, with a front-mounted 4-cylinder power unit, heavy artillery wheels, and front-facing seats for four. One or two makers still stood out for the traditional surrey or buggy shape—Olds had made his famous Curved-Dash until 1904–5 and marques such as the Kiblinger held on until 1909, but the automobile's shape was becoming established in its more conventional form.

Originators

Although the Duryea is credited as the first commercially made car in the United States, Ransom Eli Olds is generally said to be the first to set up business as a genuine manufacturer. Olds' first venture, with the aid of a couple of hundred thousand dollars from a backer, was a flat failure, until he realized that he was making too pricey a product (at $1,250 in 1899 it represented half the cost of new house) and moved from Lansing to Detroit, where he commenced work on the Curved Dash runabout.

Above Looking deceptively frail, a 1902 Curved Dash Olds copes with traffic of the 'seventies on the annual rally from London to Brighton.

Right Pioneer U.S. electric. A 1901 Columbia; this one was supplied to England's Queen Alexandra under the British factor's name of *City and Suburban*. The Queen used it only in the grounds of her home at Sandringham.

The Curved Dash was much more to the American taste of 1901; with a compact 66-inch wheelbase and weighing only 700 lbs, it had a one-cylinder 7 h.p. engine with two forward speeds and reverse, and a five-gallon fuel tank. Its wheel track was said to have been designed to fit into the cart-ruts cut into the roads of the day. Its price, kept down by a form of mass-production later to be developed to the ultimate by Henry Ford, was $650 and what more could a progressive American want?

Olds sold 425 Curved Dash cars in 1901, 3,750 in 1902, 5,000 in 1903 and 5,508 in 1904. Two of them became the first cars to compete in a U.S. transcontinental race in 1905, proving to a still-sceptical section of the public that they could survive the battering of the rough dirt roads of the day. An earlier headline had been achieved when an Olds 'Pirate' had established a world record of five miles in $6\frac{1}{2}$ minutes at Daytona. Olds wanted to continue building his Curved Dash machine but his financial backer disagreed. Olds left, started the Reo company, and the firm of Oldsmobile went on to become one of the founder members of General Motors, set up in 1908.

Detroit was a quiet, peaceful town. Nobody would have guessed in 1900 that it was destined to become one of the world's great automotive centres. But in Detroit there was one saloon in which cars were the main topic. Round a glass of beer, Ransom Olds, Henry Ford, David Buick, Henry Leland and others would talk about the empires they would build. These were no pipe-dreams, for the four men were to develop organizations that were to influence production methods and designs of the motor car throughout the world. Leland was older than the others, and came into the motor world later than them. Ford and others had started their new ventures by the time Henry Leland had found a backer prepared to finance his manufacturing plans—which he based on the principle of quality, of production and parts so accurately manufactured that they were easily interchangeable. This was a new concept then; cars were made by craftsmen, and each part, made more or less individually, would fit beautifully—but only with the specific part that had been made to mate with it. Leland's principle of changeable spares necessitated rethinking production methods and deliberately manufacturing all similar parts to a much closer tolerance than normal. Thus, Leland was the first to use methods which helped ensure the future success of the motor industry in the U.S.A.

The Henry Ford Company called Leland in to help re-organize production (superintendent Henry had already left in a huff because the boss thought he was obsessed with motor racing) and the firm was renamed

Above A 1903 2-cylinder 20 h.p. two-seater Winton.

Below Saturday afternoon parade at Detroit, 1910. Paved roads were common enough in urban regions, but abruptly changed to mud when the sidewalk ended.

the Cadillac Automobile Company in 1902, with production methods aligned to Henry Leland's principles of quality and precision.

The arrival of the Cadillac was an important addition to the American motor industry, bringing with it new standards of work. The Model A came off the line during the year of the company's foundation, a high-quality 6½ h.p. car, but the most famous Caddy of Edwardian days was undoubtedly the 'Thirty' first seen in 1908. With a 30 h.p. four separately-cast copper-water-jacket cylinder engine of about 4 litres, 75,000 were sold. An important year for Cadillac, and for the motoring public, was 1912 when the company equipped its automobiles with electric lights and starter. The search for an automatic starter had been going on for some years, with unsuccessful attempts to use compressed air, electricity and clockwork. Then Henry Leland called in engineer Charles Kettering, who had worked for the National Cash Register Company on several of their products. Kettering had designed a small electric motor to operate the cash register when a sale was made. It did not have to carry a continuous load, but work in short, high bursts of power. It was tailor-made as a starter motor, and using a generator to charge the battery between spurts of power, was first demonstrated on a Cadillac car on 27 February 1911. Several American historians have stated that this single development was not only responsible for women taking their places behind the steering wheel, but also for the change of fashion from long to shorter skirts.

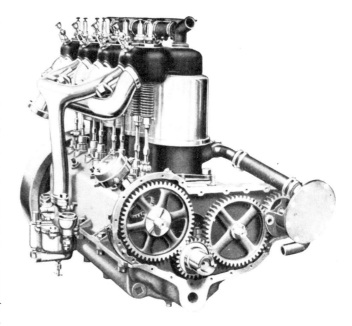

Above Power unit of the famous Cadillac 'Thirty', introduced by Henry Leland in 1906. Its four separately cast and water-jacketed cylinders had a capacity of around 4 litres.

Below The thrill of owning a new car plus the excitement of wedding-day celebrations. Supporting the guests is a 1909 Rambler.

The first cross-country race in America, staged by Oldsmobile in 1905. These two Curved Dash models battled for 44 days across the continent.

Before the twentieth century was half-a-dozen years old, American flair for innovation and development had begun to show. Their motor industry showed the way to the rest of the world in the matter of building cars in large numbers, a feat made possible by conquering the technique of consistent accuracy in the production of metal parts and by splitting the various processes of making and assembling the hundreds of parts, so that each man had to learn only a single job which could be brought to him on a moving conveyor. Hailed then as a great advance, the benefits of this type of mass-production are only now being questioned, some 70 years after mass-production made its first appearance.

However, today's automotive world owes a debt to the early American pioneers in this field, and to those of earlier days, whose crude but sturdy vehicles, made not as pleasure vehicles for the rich, but designed as utilitarian transport for the ordinary man, eventually brought motoring to us all.

Top left The first Hudson, 1909. A 20 h.p. 4-cylinder car of solid and conventional layout, it was capable of about 50 m.p.h.

Left Up to the axles in mud and snow, a 20 h.p. Regal, circa 1910. One of the hazards of early American motoring.

Above Rural America 1902. A Type 8 Autocar, with a $3\frac{1}{2}$ h.p. 2-cylinder motor and shaft drive. It looked like a good way to attract the girls.

RELIABILITY AND RACE

By 1900, the year of Britain's 1,000 Mile Trial, motor sport had been established in Europe and America for at least five years, and indeed was already one of the fashionable pursuits for the young man-about-town with an eye on fame, fortune and the ladies. Competitive events were themselves generating more interest in domestic and commercial motoring, and the whole business was escalating rapidly—to the delight of Daimler, Benz, Mors, Panhard, Peugeot, de Dion, Bollée, Duryea, Olds, Winton and others. . . .

The first motor contest, a shake-rattle-and-roll affair called a 'Reliability Trial' from Paris to Rouen, soon developed into a free-for-all race at about bicycle pace—indeed it was paced by a cyclist reporter all the way—and proved several interesting points. That petrol was more reliable than steam was perhaps the most obvious; half the steamers broke down, compared with a much smaller number *hors de combat* in the internal combustion engine category. It proved that the car could (if only just) be of use as serious transport. And it proved a sharp boost for French motor manufacturers, a boost which they could hardly wait to repeat. So to the Paris–Bordeaux race (a genuine race this time) in 1895.

Emile Levassor, in his own Panhard-Levassor, won this race—long and gruelling even by today's standards—by covering the entire distance of 732 miles in 48 hours 42 minutes, disdaining to allow his relief driver to take the wheel at all. This race landmarked the first use, by the brothers Michelin, of pneumatic tyres in competition, fitted to a Peugeot. The event illustrated that a motor could operate over long-distance routes, that air-filled tyres were an (almost) practical proposition, and that again, the petrol engine was more reliable and portable than steam power. Of the 22 to depart, the first 10 to arrive back at the Place d'Armes at Versailles were powered by petrol engines.

Motor sport in its several forms then experienced a popular explosion. Motor clubs were formed in several countries, and the sport soon became international, with events crossing national borders. Newspaper proprietor Gordon Bennett offered the first 'international' cup, a trophy for a series of races that began with a long haul from Paris to Lyon in 1900—won by the marque that led them all, a French Panhard–Levassor.

The second Gordon Bennett Cup race was run concurrently with the Paris–Bordeaux event in 1901, and this event was won by a 60 h.p. Mors. The average speed was a creditable 50 m.p.h., which, when compared with Levassor's 15 m.p.h., for the Paris–Bordeaux race of 1895, well illustrated the tremendous progress made by the automotive engineers of early motoring days.

The 1902 race was held within the famous Paris–Vienna race. The Gordon Bennett Cup event, run from Paris to Innsbrück, and won by British driver Selwyn Edge in a 30 h.p. Napier, was overshadowed by the near-incredible win in a small Renault by Marcel Renault, brother of Louis, founder of the company. His 3-litre car (small for those days of ever-growing engine capacities) arrived at the finishing post in Vienna two hours before the winner was thought due—and he had considerable difficulty in persuading early officials that he was indeed Marcel Renault from France and that he was the victor in that he had arrived first, before the great Panhards, Mercedes and Mors. Particularly the Mercedes, for whom the Viennese had prepared an enthusiastic reception. . . .

The country-to-country, open-road racing of the early 1900s came to an abrupt halt in 1903, when the Paris-Madrid race ended in carnage, killing five competitors and several spectators in a series of horrific accidents. Racing speeds had risen so acutely, engines had ballooned out to such vast litreage, frames had been pared and drilled out so near to collapsing point to get a better power-to-weight ratio, that the whole thing had become a nightmare for the drivers who could now travel at 80 m.p.h. plus, and a death-trap for spectators who, knowing little of the hazards of speeding vehicles, crowded the edges of the routes.

A First for the U.S.A.

The first motoring competition to be seen by the public in the United States was the Chicago–Evanston contest, promoted in 1895 by the Chicago Times Herald. It was a flop—only two cars, a Duryea and a Benz were ready by race-day—so it was re-run on Thanksgiving Day that year.

Snow and ice made the race, shortened to 54 miles because of the weather conditions, something of a miniature Monte Carlo Rally (an event to be mounted for the first time 16 years later) and this time six entrants

Top right Waiting in a vine-covered courtyard for the start of the Paris to Rouen trial in 1894. The first motor sport event soon changed from reliability trial to race. This is a Peugeot phaeton.

Right Germany favoured trials rather than races in pioneer days, so that competitors' vehicles bore closer relation to catalogue cars. Here is a Fiat photographed during the 1906 Herkomer Trials.

lined up on the cold and slippery start-line. Frank Duryea won the race, although there is still some controversy about this point, in his second car in which he had put a four-cycle engine. This win for the 'original' U.S. carmakers, the Duryea Motor Wagon Company, although it caused no great stir in transport circles at the time, opened the gates to motor sport in the U.S.A.

Various cross-country events took place in America after that essay into the sport, but the first big sporting series of significance in the early 1900s was the Vanderbilt Cup. Willie K. Vanderbilt had been interested in several sports—horses, boats—and had finally become fascinated by the motor car and had driven in some of the dangerous European capital-to-capital events. His avowed purpose in mounting the series was 'to encourage the development of the automobile in the United States' and one cannot help supposing that there may have been an element of 'we can do better than Europe' in his attitude.

The Long Island route for the race ensured that it was watched by a maximum number of people—over 30,000 attended the first one, held on 8 October 1904—and some of them narrowly missed a sticky end. The crowd's knowledge of motor racing was nil, and the marshalling of the watchers was minimal. Cars that were travelling at up to 60 m.p.h. rattled over washboard level crossings, tipping out their drivers; other

competitors dodged chickens and children in dramatic slaloms, buckled their vehicles on corners or lost their engines over rutted sections, and to a man were terrified by the packed masses who behaved with all the suicidal habits of the Paris–Madrid fans. A French–American driver, George Heath, won the 284-mile race in a Panhard at 52.2 m.p.h.

However the Vanderbilt Cup wasn't to be stopped by a little blood. Drivers learned, so did spectators. And in 1905 it was held again—and was highly successful in terms of interest and attendance. In true American style, the event, already the automotive social occasion of the season, was further popularized by a Broadway Musical of the same name. The names of the cars still had a continental ring, Panhard, Mercedes, Renault, and so on, though gradually over the years the entry began to change its content to names like Pope-Toledo, Simplex, Packard—American marques that attracted even larger and more partisan audiences.

Until 1908 the Vanderbilt Cup held sports fans spellbound, then, as racing in other parts of the world became more sophisticated and engines started to shrink, the vast cars of Vanderbilt days no longer produced the best in racing, and the interest moved over to the new American Grand Prize, a new race that conformed to the European engine-size regulations of 117 sq. ins. piston area. It naturally attracted European manufacturers and drivers, and a pot-hunting Fiat won,

followed by a Benz. Grand Prix formula changed in 1912 to a Formula Libre (any capacity) but the Vanderbilt Cup was by this time an ailing event and although run on the same circuit as the American Grand Prize was no longer the focal point of interest.

In Europe

Similar ill fortune was suffered by the Gordon Bennett Cup in Europe. Why, said the French (who had more motor manufacturers than anyone else, and wanted the world to know it) should we be restricted to an entry of three cars from France in the race, just like any small one-car producing country? They had a case—and implemented it by organizing a race of their own in 1906 under new regulations. Held at Le Mans on a new 103 kilometre closed circuit, it was called the Grand Prix de l'Automobile Club de France, or just the Grand Prix, and was a major turning point in motor sporting history.

Top left Next year, once again. The Paris-Bordeaux race was won by Emile Levassor in this Panhard-Levassor. He drove the entire 732 miles of the route himself.

Far left Another race that has become established in motoring lore, the 1902 Paris-Vienna event, won by Marcel Renault. Here (in cap and beard) he relaxes after winning at an average of 39 m.p.h.

Above Two Opel brothers were already famous as competition drivers by the time another Opel, Wilhelm, won the 1909 Prince Henry Trial in Germany. This is the winning 10/20 h.p. Opel, still bearing the muddy marks of victory.

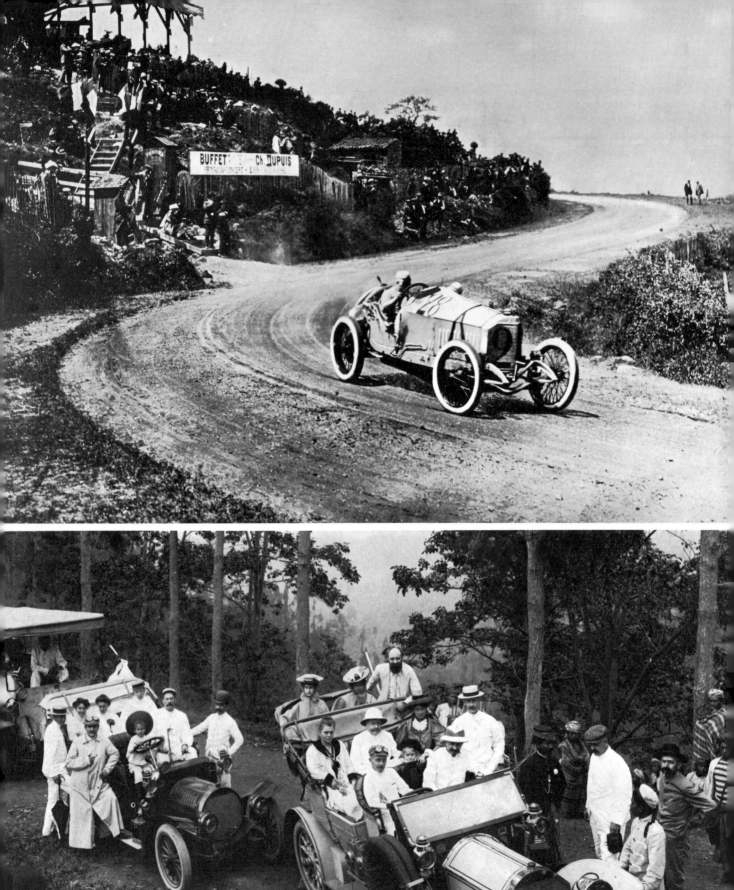

It was a race to remember. A contest between Italy, Germany and France. Italy had three Fiats, Germany six cars—and France had entered no fewer than 23 cars of ten different marques. With vehicles clocking over 90 m.p.h. in rising temperatures and rapidly melting tar—laid to hold down the dust but presenting an even nastier hazard—and with road surfaces rough enough to cause a couple of punctures a lap, the first French Grand Prix was no picnic. No restrictions on engine capacity were in force and some of the monsters bred by this situation were formidable indeed, brake horsepower ranging up to 130 and engine sizes up to a massive 18 litres.

This race of Edwardian dinosaurs was won by a 90 h.p. Renault, one of the marques that had fitted another new Michelin development, detachable wheel rims. And in a race in which at least one competitor had to change his entire set of tyres *ten times* this innovation was quite a comfort to those who had elected to use it.

Racing these overblown monsters went on for a few years but by 1914, the brute-force-and-bigger-motors brigade were beginning to lose out to the (comparatively) smaller-engined vehicles of more advanced type for it was in 1914 that another historic turning point in the blood-and-thunder story of motor sport was reached. Again it was the classic Grand Prix de l'Automobile Club de France, the sixth in the series,

Top left End of an era—the 1914 French Grand Prix. Here Christian Lautenschlager, Mercedes driver and eventual winner, takes a sharp bend in the Lyon circuit.

Left Motor sport the social way. The leading car is a 28/40 h.p. 'triple phaeton' designed for the larger Italian family. The picture shows a meeting of the Java Motor Club, 1910.

Below Le Mans, 1927. The race was won this year by a Bentley driven by British driver 'Sammy' Davis and co-driver J. D. Benjafield after suffering a crippling crash. Here Benjafield (right) overtakes a Schneider.

and that year held at a venue outside Lyon. This time there were 30 competitors, with a much more even distribution of countries and marques. Germany was there with Mercedes and Opel teams, Britain with Vauxhall and Sunbeam, Italy with Fiat, France with Peugeot (winners of the 1912 and 1913 races with Georges Boillot at the wheel) and Delage as main French hopes; their four-wheel brakes would give them an edge over the others, it was thought.

The Peugeot's four-wheel brakes certainly persuaded the motor industry that the rear-wheels-only variety had had their day—but they did not win the race for the favourite, Boillot. He was goaded into cracking up his Peugeot by the Mercedes team tactics, part of which was to sacrifice one of their cars by chasing the Frenchman into the ground.

L'Endurance

Grand Prix racing—in effect the term then meant the French Grand Prix—was an established part of motor sport before World War I, but there were those who saw that the cars, fast becoming so specialized, would inevitably lose the lay-public's interest as they developed farther and farther away from normal road vehicle design and performance.

Several years earlier, in 1907, Sicilian Vincenzo Florio had promoted a road race on his island which in fact represented the continuation of races similar to the long road marathons that ceased with the Paris-Madrid event. But the 24 Hours Endurance race at Le Mans was born because, by 1922, racing had fulfilled pre-war forecasts and had indeed become so esoteric that many of the former race-attending enthusiasts were drifting away. A race that would show the virtues of standard vehicles, which the growing motoring public could recognize as catalogue cars, was necessary to bring them back. So the Le Mans 24 Hour race was designed, at

first, around three main rules: that the cars should be standard purchasable products, that they should carry touring coachwork, and that all (except those with less than 1100 c.c. engines) should have four-seater bodies. It proved an excellent move and the crowds flocked to the Sarthe circuit, from the date of the first race in May 1923, until the 24 Hours of Le Mans became a national Derby Day for a quarter million French motor sport fans.

The Italian classic, the Mille Miglia, first run three years after Le Mans began, was probably engendered by the rapid success of the French race. The thousand-mile dash round half Italy in the style of the old inter-city road marathons quickly acquired a cachet, and a large international following, despite the fact that the characteristics of the route favoured home drivers, and for the first dozen years it was won by Italians in Italian cars, except in 1931 when it was a German benefit.

Above The Type 35B Bugatti of 1926, the period when the sport turned to Formule Libre to escape the meagre 1½-litre Grand Prix limit.

Right Still circulating—a 3·3-litre Talbot from the end of the Vintage period, 1930.

Grand Prix Formulae

In 1902 a maximum weight of 1,000 kilogrammes (the first 'Formula' regulation) was laid down for international events, and enforced until the end of the 1906 season. The Grand Prix Formula then changed as follows:

1907	Upper limit of fuel consumption 9.4 m.p.g.
1908	Bore restricted to 155 mm for a 4-cylinder engine
1912	Formula Libre (unlimited capacity)
1914	Engine size restricted to 4½ litres unsupercharged.
1921	Engine size restricted to 3 litres.
1922–5	Engine size restricted to 2 litres.
1926–7	Engine size restricted to 1½ litres.
1928–33	Formula Libre (engines size unrestricted, weight limits from 550 kg to 750 kg: minimum race distance of 600 kilometres.

THE EDWARDIANS

Britain's King Edward VII, of the dynasty of Saxe-Coburg, died aged 68 in 1910, neatly ending the short Edwardian Age on a round figure. For the motoring world however, vehicles classed as Edwardian range from 1905 to 1918. The first date is logical enough, it was around this time that automobilists realized that they were a permanent, if not universally welcome part of the scene, and others, not yet fully acquainted with the delights of motoring, began to observe that the motor car was not only the transport of the uncertain future, but indeed was starting to play a serious role in the present. The later limiting date eight years into the reign of George V, covers what could be called an Edwardian attitude to car-manufacturing and motoring, and was set by the Veteran Car Club of Great Britain.

In 1903, an Act of Parliament had been passed—the first of real motoring significance since the great charter of 1896—stating the ways in which motorists must abide by the laws, detailed penalties for such modern misdemeanours as driving on a public highway in manner 'reckless or negligent'; warned motorists not to forge their own licences, and outlined accident procedure. And in a later section, the Act gave the daredevil motorist his way in a verbal backhander stating that 'a person shall not, under any circumstances, drive a motor car on the public highway at a speed exceeding 20 miles an hour (eight extra m.p.h. on the clock, no less!). The green light had been given, and the Edwardian motorist drank of the heady freedom of the roads, a nectar tainted only by the running battle with local hedge-hiding constabulary.

On the world motoring scene movement was rapid and often dramatic. By 1906 the car was long past its experimental stage; as a French writer said this was an 'epoch of consolidation', during which the direction of effort had moved from making the thing work, to making it work well. Gone were the days when the vehicle was introduced by advertisements directed to *The Nobility and Gentry* running, for example, like this one of 1896: *This novel vehicle is propelled by an* INTERNAL COMBUSTION ENGINE *of 2 cylinder and 6 horse power, relying on petroleum for its motive power, and will attain the comfortable speed of 12 miles per hour on the level, etc. etc.* By 1906 almost all cars were enclosed and chauffeured, and travel was silent and smooth. Daimler of Coventry were offering a fine 9¼ litre 35 h.p. car to the discerning public, increasing numbers of public buses were mechanically driven, cars had been used to convey voters to a general election in Britain, continental motoring holidays were fashionable for the Edwardian rich. Lanchester, Crossley, Dennis, Horbick, Humber were names to buy. American Wilbur Gunn had opened a factory in Staines near London and was making a car called Lagonda, the aristocratic Napier was seen about town in its 6-cylinder glory, and three new Rolls-Royces had been on offer by the Hon. Charles Rolls for a year, the first 40/50 Silver Ghost was due to be seen at the autumn Motor Show, and a four-wheel braked Mercedes had appeared.

Transport for (almost) All

Moneyed society dictated what the car should offer the purchaser, right through from the beginning to the end of the Edwardian motoring era. In 1905 if you hunted, then you may well have owned a motor car; if you were on the upper rungs of a profession, you may *just* have owned a car; if you were anything else—not a hope. Price was, to a large degree, irrelevant; £350 for a 1905 10 h.p. De Dion was so far beyond the pocket of the average citizen (it could represent two year's salary) that only those whose wealth permitted them to ignore cost could play the motoring game.

Servicing could occupy an hour or two a day, there was petrol to be bought and carried from ironmonger or chemist, brass to be polished, spare parts to be blacksmithed, as often as not out of blanks. Not to have a chauffeur would be unthinkable. But when one noble peer actually had the front compartment of his Delaunay-Belleville fitted with weather-proof side-screens to protect his investment in a skilled driver the motoring *grand monde* was astonished.

In the United States the picture was markedly different—the automobile was made for the people. Most were considerably less refined than European cars. Duryea had been selling buggies for ten years, and by 1906 the company offered a large 3-cylinder 25 h.p. car and other smaller models, some still steered by tiller.

In 1906, Henry Ford, after a chequered start, was now running through the model-alphabet and making his luxury 6-cylinder Model K, selling at $2,400 and costing him more than that figure to make! His 1906 Model N, however, rivalled the Oldsmobile in price and popularity (the Oldsmobile twin-cylinder 2-stroke engine had just found its way to the front of the car) and led to the greatest of them all, the Model T, in a couple of years.

A 12-cylinder horizontal-engined flywheel-less Maxwell, and a 120 h.p. Pope-Toledo (looking very like

a European tourer) using some odd engineering principles, not least of which was the sharing of a single valve spring between each set of two valves, were entered for the 1906 Vanderbilt Cup, as were the Thomas entries, dead ringers for the French Brasiers and highly conventional for the time. But most of the cars of America still appeared to be designed by delightful eccentrics, and the layout had not yet settled down as it had in Europe after (some considerable time after) Emile Levassor's front-engined design.

However, during the later years of the first decade of the twentieth century American designers shook off the bicycle-and-buggy influence, and at last the tiller reluctantly disappeared and engines began to emerge from under the passenger seat and move to the forward end of the car. The industry was slowly attracted towards Detroit, drawn by its geographical and distribution advantages—and the fact the Olds had been forced to farm out parts-manufacturing after a fire way back in 1901 when a single Curved Dash had survived. Some of these parts-makers had by 1906, become manufacturers in their own right, and in turn drew others to the Michigan town. . . .

In two years time General Motors was to be formed, merging Cadillac, Olds, Buick and the Oakland Motor Car Company of Pontiac Michigan to create the nucleus of a group that was in years to come, to employ nearly a million people in the United States, Britain, Germany and Australia. In 1906 most American roads were still miserable tracks, better suited to horses than the emergent auto, but although it had taken two months for a car to travel from San Francisco to New York in 1903, by 1906 cars were becoming more reliable and had long lost that straight-out-of-the-egg look. The Wright brothers had flown at Kitty Hawk a couple of years back, and by 1912, in six years time, an airplane was to cross the country in a total flying time of $3\frac{1}{2}$ days.

By 1912 Cadillac had made history by being the first company to fit electric self-starters, lighting and ignition, and the automotive industry made history that year by producing over 350,000 motor cars.

By 1916, the entire way of life had changed in America. The age of the handcraft product was past, rural communities were shifting to the big towns, the numbers of horses used as transport had dwindled and the pace of life had greatly increased. Cars and aircraft were beginning to pour out of the factories in ever-larger numbers, Ford had been making his Tin Lizzie, the Model T, for eight years and in 1916 used it as a basis for a tractor design, bringing mechanization to the vast farmlands of the country. Chevrolet in 1916 were rivalling Ford with the 2.7 litre 4-cylinder '490', offering it at the price of its name. The car sold well—and was continued with minor changes for six years. Ironically, and luckily, America had geared up so rapidly for mass-production of mechanical goods—not only in the motor field—that the country was well equipped, if not well prepared, for the war that she was to enter in 1917.

Below The Rover Company produced this 8 h.p. model in 1906. A similar car was used by R. L. Jefferson for his epic journey to Turkey in 1905–6.

. . . Carry a Small Revolver

Edwardian Britain presented a different scene, more cushioned by wealth, more leisured in pace. Motoring was the prerogative still of those who had erstwhile been 'carriage-trade' and in whose mind the machines they now conducted were naturally restricted to people who had the intelligence to use them with discretion and care.

However, if this was a typical example of the motorist's attitude to his driving there was an occasional lack of the proper restraint . . . leading to verses, cartoons, lampoons and the like in journals such as Punch, a magazine that had already urged in its own ironic way, that all horses be preceded by a man with a red flag, and which had before the turn of the century forecast a 'Motor Derby'; for example:

I collided with some trippers in my swift de Dion Bouton,
Squashed them out as flat as kippers, left them 'aussi mort que mouton',
What a nuisance trippers are, I must now repaint the car . . .
(and so on) by which one assumes that that very British journal was already aware of the type of driver that would be seen on public roads in the not-too-distant future.

Right Lord Montagu and party speed down the Brighton Road in a 24 h.p. 1903 De Dietrich tonneau.

Below Thornycroft 20 h.p. 4-cylinder double phaeton, 1903, the epitome of Edwardian style. This car belonged to Mr Tom Thornycroft, one of the company's founders, until 1957.

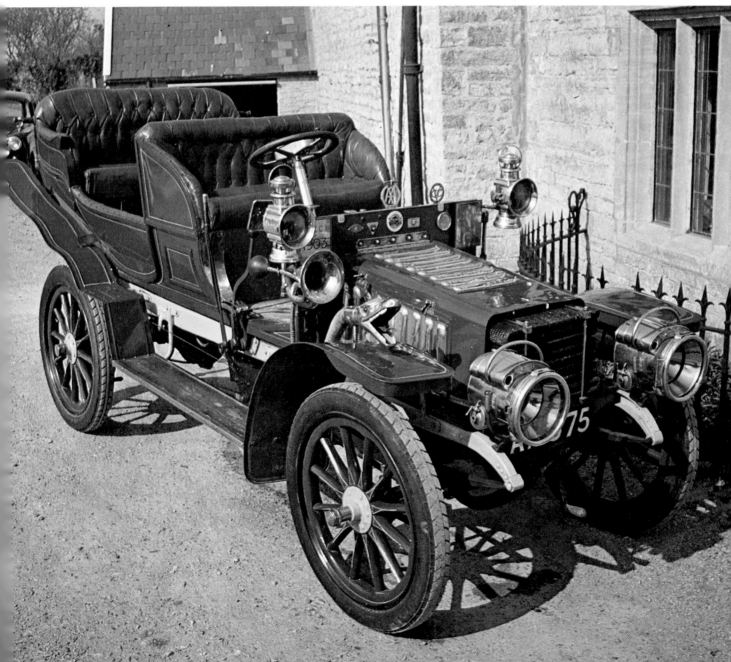

DEA EX MACHINÂ. THE GODDESS OUT OF THE CAR.

"But what is this? What thing of sea or land?
Female of sex it seems,
That so bedecked, ornate, and gay,
Comes this way, sailing
Like a stately ship.

  ⁑   ⁑   ⁑   ⁑   ⁑   ⁑

An amber scent of odoriferous perfume
Her harbinger."—MILTON, *Samson Agonistes.*

Top Published in Punch, 1902.

Above Monsieur Sabattier's designs for the automobilist of the early twentieth century.

New motoring journals had hatched and thrived in the early part of the century and were now open to motoring correspondence, their columns brimming with advice on driving and the cost of running a car with or without a chauffeur. Fashion features offered new ways of coping with dusty roads and open cars, whilst retaining a degree of elegance (this must have been one of the most difficult and confusing fashion periods in history), and as cars became more enclosed leaving only the employed driver to catch pneumonia in his exposed front seat, fashions for madame were centred on what to wear whilst being admired by the populace through the car's large glass windows.

Consider this fashion note of the early Edwardian epoch: 'The pleasure of automobiling in the winter is spoiled if one's face and ears are unprotected. The Scott chest and ear muffler makes freezing weather pleasant. It is warm and dressy, and can be folded and put in the coat pocket when not in use'. And looked extraordinarily like a World War I gasmask, too. Then there was the 'Motoring Collar' which the writer describes as 'an excellent stock collar . . . made of white canvas similar to the material of which stocks for hunting are made, retains its firmness even after a long day's motoring in hot weather, a fact which gives the wearer an enormous advantage over those who use the ordinary starched lined collars which are apt to become deplorably limp . . .'.

Other columnists in the ladies' glossies suggest open-car travellers wear 'straw hats in the French sailor style, and a good face mask with two mica eyepieces', an anti-dust fashion much worn by early female passengers and one which could strike terror into bucolic onlookers.

Said Lady Jeune, another early woman driver, in the national press; 'A lady sitting entirely exposed to the elements and to the rude stares of passing pedestrians, must be prepared to sacrifice her femininity. The fact that women should motor, and care for it as they do, is a great tribute to their lack of personal vanity, for it is almost impossible to make the dress they have to wear, a becoming one. There are two things only to be considered: how a woman can keep herself warm in winter, and not be suffocated by dust in the summer without making herself very unattractive.'

Writes Miss Dorothy Levitt (who was, in 1906, to set up a woman's world record of 91 m.p.h.): 'If you are to drive alone on the highways and byways it is advisable to carry a small revolver. I have an automatic Colt and find it easy to handle as there is practically no recoil, a great consideration to a woman'.

For the man at the wheel there was the 'Spring-belt robe' a piece of apparel almost guaranteed to cause unspeakable injuries to the wearer. Its secret, said the advertising copy, 'lies in a belt of fine tempered spring steel, open at the back, made to the shape of the body. Its resiliency makes it adaptable to the use of persons of any size, and holds the robe in place . . . so that it can be instantly removed with one pull at the front'. Anything

Late Edwardian days in Coventry. A 1911 Daimler in Butcher Row. This car is fitted with a contemporary 'side-slip' safety device, a single studded tyre on the front offside wheel.

USE ROSS PETROL

!!! This is The Best and Most Economical Motor Spirit in the Market, and it is Home Made.

Manufactured by
JAMES ROSS & Cº, Philpstoun Oil Works, Linlithgow, NB.

Above Ross, a company which became part of Scottish Oils (later part of BP) advertises in 1906. Petrol was still stocked by iron-mongers.

nearer to a straightjacket one could not get, and the consequences of the one pull at the front could, one imagines, be disastrous.

So for the early cold-motoring fraternity, furs, goggles, masks, footwarmers, robes that enveloped like a wigwam, giant mackintoshes, electrically-heated gloves and the like were the vogue, and without exception were heavy, cumbersome and hideous.

Happily, enforced open motoring gave way eventually, first to the touring hood, and then to the saloon or sedan; but the early Edwardians really suffered, before some bright designer thought of all-round passenger protection against inclement weather. Curiously, nobody seemed to remember that Louis Renault had done it in 1899, with his sedan-chair type saloon.

Lady Driver

Even before the invention of the electric self-starter, certain hardy ladies were to be seen at the wheel. Although most considered it altogether too daring to be seen in a motor car without an escort, a Ladies Automobile Club had been formed by 1905 and one prominent lady driver was interviewed by the Lady's Pictorial, which described her as, 'Mrs. Edward Kennard—a pioneer automobilist, a daring rider, and an expert wielder of the rod'. Fishing rod, of course. The report mirrored the adventurous spirit of the time when it quoted Mrs. K. She was asked if she preferred the hunting field to motoring: 'I enjoy both equally well,' the lady replied. 'Neither interferes with the pursuit of the other. One hunts in cold damp weather and when it is dry and hot, one motors. I like my motors as much as my horses, they present so many problems to solve, like all mechanisms, and to solve problems—to dive into the unknown—is delightful.'

'Changing tyres,' said Mrs. Kennard, 'needs considerable exercise of muscular strength; pumping up is a big business and I took fully 200 strokes to inflate my husband's Napier.' Could she carry out running repairs? Indeed she could, at least on a motor-cycle,

'such as shortening, removing and putting on belts, grinding valves, attending to the ignition and carburettor.' Some running repairs . . . and some lady driver!

A true Edwardian 'Automobilist' Mrs. Kennard was even then a trifle conservative, in the way she still considered motoring a pastime. Others were using the now accepted transport for work and the routine of daily life. Smaller and less expensive cars were coming on the market. The classified advertisement columns were full of private transactions, vignettes that today reveal much about the Edwardian attitude to the automobile, although some of them have a modern ring. This one for instance, printed in The Motor, 13 June 1905: 'SWIFT 5½ h.p. light car, detachable back seat and tyres as new, very little used, what offers? Or exchange tricar and cash. Motorist, Church St., Swadlincote.'

Another that would make the modern collector bite his nails and wish he had been born half a century earlier runs: '6 h.p. Panhard-Levassor, suit officer or doctor, three speeds and reverse, in thorough order. £70 or nearest offer. Barnett, 13 Norfolk Road, Erdington, Birmingham. It was probably one of the Panhards bought new from the agency of the Hon. Charles Rolls, before his fateful meeting with Henry Royce in 1904.

This one is something of a prestige sale: 'WOLSELEY 10 h.p. magnificent car, four speeds and reverse, tonneau body, splendid order, painted black and yellow, complete with detachable hood, large leather guards, all spare parts, plated Bleriot lamp and plated side and tail lamps, lowest £105. R. Warrilow, Shirley, Ellenborough Park, Weston-super-Mare.' Splendid indeed, and one can well imagine that black and yellow car gliding smoothly and disdainfully along the prom of Weston to the admiration of the trippers and envy of the locals. By the time the advert was placed it was probably three or four years old—the 10 h.p. Herbert Austin-designed 2.6-litre Wolseley flat-twin which sold new for £360. A fine car—had not Queen Alexandra bought a Wolseley in 1903? And as wife of England's premier automobilist she should know how to choose a car.

The Royal Motorist

The King had been a motorist for some time—a Daimler man, of course, but both his ancestry and the fact that the Daimler was now a truly British product made this quite proper. He had bought his first car in 1900, a Daimler phaeton now called the 'Sandringham' model, and had added from time to time to his stable. As the distinguished motoring-society magazine The Car fanfared with pomp more appropriate to a Royal birth, on 7 January 1903: 'We have pleasure in announcing that His Majesty has this week decided to add to his

Right Opel 10/18 h.p. double phaeton of 1909. Opel's earlier Kaiserpreis successes influenced the development of this model.

stud of cars. It may be remembered that . . . he had also ordered another car to be constructed for the use of his loaders.'

The car was a 22 h.p. 4-cylinder Daimler with seating for no less than 14. As the specifications said: 'The body and wheels are to be of dark and light oak, with "natural wood" finish. A canopy top will be provided for light luggage. Goodyear pneumatic tyres will be fitted to the front wheels . . . special (brass bound) cartridge boxes will be supplied with the car, to be fitted under the seats . . . The fact that His Majesty has again ordered an English-built car is not only a tribute to the Daimler firm itself but also to British industry; indeed we may state that His Majesty is thoroughly well pleased with his motor vehicles and has definitely declared that he will never have an automobile of foreign manufacture.' A declaration to which the Royal Family adhered for around half a century.

The motoring press of the day was very much a two-way communication medium, as it is today. New drivers would offer their opinions on much the same subjects that are found in their columns now, some as bitter—some as highly technical, others just as fatuous . . .

'Does not commonsense dictate that amateur, as well as professional drivers be licenced to drive the motor cars?' asks one inquiring mind, 'for the more skilled the driver (amateur?) the greater the tendency to excessive speeds.' To which the answer was: 'Is there not always a sufficiently deterrent influence in the fact that a man who is the owner will not willingly do anything to wreck his car by careless management? And again if the amateur is unskilled he will wreck his car in a thousand ways before he becomes a public danger.' Curious logic in retrospect.

Then a useful little filler of a type often seen tucked into the corners of pages, 'Mr. H. W. Bartleet of Nottingham warns automobilists that the road between Bletchingly and Redhill is under repair, and should be avoided for the present'.

A disappointed motorist writes in 1905: 'Sir, I have a 12 h.p. Darracq car, 1904, but I am not satisfied with the mileage per gallon of petrol obtained. I should like to hear opinions from readers, and other owners of the same car as to the possible reason. One engine throws the lubricating oil past the piston rings, and into the valves, which the companion engine does not do, and yet the compression is about equal. Yours faithfully A.E.' This was the year of the 3.1 litre Flying 15 Darracq

Below Charabanc outings for the populace. A car of his own was not part of even the wildest dreams of the ordinary man-in-the-street in Edwardian times, but this was one way in which horizons could be widened.

Top right Edwardian military exercises, 1909. An experiment in mobility for a battalion of Guards proved highly successful when they were conveyed from London to Hastings by A.A. members.

Bottom right Rolls-Royce at War, 1916. This light armoured car had three-eighths-inch armour, and mounted a single machine gun. 'A Rolls in the desert is above rubies,' said T. E. Lawrence during his Arabian campaign against the Turks.

with its one-piece pressed steel frame and which had, according to the brochure, only one engine. . . .

An *Autocar* snippet, 1902: 'Automobilism is spreading apace, especially in London. Last week a member of our staff, whilst in the West End, counted twenty-three cars within three-quarters of an hour.' By 1910, there were to be 142,000 of them, mostly in the London area. . . .

Another reader complained of road conditions in 1905: 'Sir, I suppose there always will be dust, but some of our road-makers manufacture it for us . . . I was astonished to see good stone being laid and the mud heaps (previously scraped from the roads) being thrown on to bind the stone! I have been smothered in dust after passing cars which are quite invisible after passing. . . .'

In a letter appealing to motorists to keep the laws of the land (particularly the new 20 m.p.h. speed limit) a reader of a leading magazine writes: 'What could be more maddening to these people (anti-motorists) than to see cars and bicycles ignoring this law and racing about at 30 m.p.h.' What indeed.

And finally a spot of advice from the expert: 'At this time of year (January) it is best to have ready in one's motor house, and stored away in glass or earthenware vessel for preference, sufficient anti-freezing solution to fill up one's water tank in case of a sudden cold snap.

Frost usually finds one unprepared. . . .' Situation normal.

And so the colourful and often elegant Edwardian age of motoring arrived at 1914, a time in Europe when motoring became—much more rapidly than expected—a matter of transporting supplies or troops to a front somewhere in Western France, a time when the keen automobilist from the upper middle class would have laid up his precious motor car for a long and cold four-year winter, and taken himself off to the war. In America the same thing happened three years later. So the days of nine-foot tall Daimlers, the first great days of Brooklands, the days when the Continent opened up like a willing oyster to the new breed of motorist, when Rolls-Royce Silver Ghosts were the envy of the world, when the tremendous ability of the aristocracy to direct their every energy to the pursuit of their new sport had quickly brought about a change in transport from horses to horsepower, came to an abrupt and tragic halt, never to be revived. . . .

Below Hispano-Suiza Alfonso, 1912. Named after the King of Spain this 3,168 c.c., 15·9 h.p. sports car could achieve 70 m.p.h. The car is now an Edwardian gem worth over twenty times its original price of £545.

Right A 1908 Hutton, one of three 4-cylinder racing-type cars built by Napier for the Tourist Trophy of that year.

Edwardian Elegance

A journal described the interior of a 1903 Mors 'Pullman' as having individual, but by no means unusual, fittings: '. . . the whole of the inside woodwork is of polished mahogany. In between these are two side tables forming small cupboards and drawers. The tops of these are polished, whilst they can be opened up to form one large table covered on the face with green baize.

'The front of the car inside (behind the driver's seat) is fitted with a morocco leather holdall, comprising clock, barometer, thermometer, manicure set, notebooks, looking glass, and an electric telephone to the drivers with an indicator marked *right, left, turn, steady, home, quicker,* etc.

'There are two electric light sprays, each having two 8 c.p. lights with glass shades, which derive their power from two sets of accumulators giving 16 volts each. These are placed in the well of the car between the driver's seats and the main body. A heating apparatus for the winter (which can be connected to the exhaust at will) is also provided.

'The ceiling is decorated in the Louis XV style, whilst the car is furnished with royal blue plush curtains and bands and the floor is covered with a dark crimson Wilton pile carpet.'

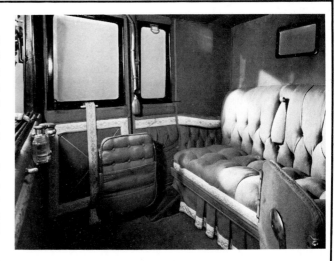

Above Button-backed plush, brocade sashes, a speaking tube to James, decanters, and roller blinds for the windows. An interior with 'individual but not unusual' fittings.

Below End of an era. The date is 1914, and A.A. scouts are taxied to the recruiting station to volunteer for active service.

Top right Edwardian to Elizabethan. This was the London-Brighton road at Merstham in 1909 . . .

Below right . . . and as it was in 1971.

FOURTH POWER~ITALY

Above Fiat No. 1, 1899. Made in the old Ceirano bicycle factory in Turin it housed a 2-cylinder 3½ h.p. motor (also optimistically called a 4 h.p at the time) with a capacity of 679 c.c. It had three forward speeds, but to go backwards, one pushed.

Below Pushing the motor car into the twentieth century—with hopeful sales background.

The early advances made towards the end of the last century in Germany puts that country historically in the forefront of the motoring story. But soon after the coincidental production of the first genuine motor cars by Benz and Daimler the centre of events moved to France, particularly when Panhard and Peugeot began production based on Daimler-licenced engines. Bollée and De Dion also helped the swing westwards, the establishing of France as the 'senior' motoring country and the language of motoring and motor sport as French. Great Britain, slow to stir, gathered its wits just as the Victorian age came to a close in 1900, and took some time to catch up with the surging developments on the continent of Europe.

On the southern side of the Alps another motor industry was laying its national foundations, mainly on the warm plains of Lombardy, in northern Italy. For Italians, Fiat is synomymous with motoring, and more Fiats are owned by people in the country of their origin, than even Volkswagen can claim in Germany.

The story of this immensely powerful company—it is the largest manufacturing organization of *any kind* in Italy—and of the motor car in Italy, begins, as has been said more than once, like the first act of a Verdi opera. Two young friends, both officers of the Savoia Cavalry regiment, lead a debonair existence in Verona in the early 'nineties. Lieutenants Giovanni Agnelli and Giulio Gropello begin several interesting experiments with an old Daimler oil engine in their lodgings at the Corso Cavour. On their way home one evening they are heard talking about Gropello's earlier inventions, an improved parachute, 'I was certain that my parachute would hold me up,' says Giulio, 'according to my calculations it was more than sufficient to suspend me in the air. Er . . . luckily the roof of the farmhouse was only two metres from the ground. Even so, I broke a leg.' And that seems to the casual observers to be much the same mood in which they construct a new carburettor for the scrap engine.

Assisted by their faithful old servant Scotto, they start up their motor—and are blown out of the workshop by the explosion. The young officers run over to Scotto who is lying on the ground looking somewhat pale. However they continue with their experiments—and at this point the opera changes to a record of success in the motor industry surpassed by very few.

With the backing of several financiers Agnelli opened up for business in 1899 in Turin, as Società Italiana per la Costruzione e il Commercio delle Automobili, Torino—happily to be abbreviated later to Fabbrica Italiana Automobili Torino, or F.I.A.T., which in 1907 dropped its stops and capitals to the somewhat ecclesiastical 'Fiat'.

Late in 1899 appeared the first of the long line of cars, made in the Ceirano bicycle factory (with which came the services of Vincenzo Lancia, who was to found his own company in seven years time, and Felice Nazzaro, later himself to race for Fiat).

A 679 c.c. single-cylinder *elegance* with a vis-à-vis
seating and a nice line in perambulator hoods, the first
Turin production could lope along at a surprising 22
m.p.h. Said the contemporary publicity: . . . *lightness, no
worry, no noise, minimum consumption, price which fears no
competition . . . a vehicle for outings, for racing, and for the
mountains.* Smart stuff, appealing to everybody and with
none of the snob overtones of most early advertisements. Number Two, in 1901, was similar, but with
one significant change, a front-engine. With its two
cylinders and 8 h.p. it made 30 m.p.h.

By the end of the year F.I.A.T. cars *looked* like
automobiles and the 12 h.p. of that year was a popular
export to France, England and the United States. No
fewer than 134 were built, a large production for the
time. The car also had a great advantage over previous
models; it housed a 4-cylinder engine. Meanwhile the
company had made several racing cars, and had, since
1900, won races in them.

From 1902 F.I.A.T. fairly leapt into production both
diverse and numerous. A 6-litre 24–32 h.p. in 1903;
4 and 4½ litre capacity models with multi-disc clutch, a
60 h.p. Corsa (racing model), which was then made as
a quality road car, then in 1905 another leap forward
when the Ansaldi works were absorbed and Fiat-
Ansaldi (Brevetti) models were brought out. In the
racing field a 16-litre giant (with overhead valves) was
born in 1905, a 110 h.p. Gordon Bennett car was built

later in the same year, a fast Targa Florio car in 1907,
and in 1911 the 4-cylinder 28,353 c.c. 300 h.p. S76
Record, a monster of incredibly ungainly shape, and
top speed of 180 m.p.h. (at Long Island in April 1912).

A Car for the Mountains

One-time book-keeper and later maker of fine cars,
Vincenzo Lancia has a place elsewhere in this book,
and since 1906 he and his company, now once again
part of Fiat, has had a prominent role in the Italian
motor story. At that same distant date Darracq, a
French company partly financed by British money,
opened its new factory at Suresnes in France and began
preparations for making its small cars in Italy. The plan
failed, mainly because of inferior parts sent out from
the French factory for assembly in the Italian works,
but also because the underpowered vehicle just could
not travel over the mountainous Italian terrain.

A group of Italian motoring enthusiasts, foreseeing
the value of an all-Italian car, bought the Darracq-
owned site at Milan, formed a company they called
A.L.F.A. (Societa Anonima Lombarda Fabbrica Auto-

Above Alpine pioneer Vincenzo Lancia in his Fiat days, reaches the
remoter parts of the country in a 24 h.p. car. Here he poses with a
Piedmontese family, 1905.

Right Tipo Zero from the Fourth Power, 1912. With 12–15 h.p.
this was the first small car to be produced by Fiat in large numbers—
over 2,000 were made within two years.

mobili) and started production in 1910 with tough 4-cylinder cars designed to climb the local Alps. The first car from the Milan works was a 2,413 c.c. 25 b.h.p., the '15/20', and a 4,084 c.c., the '20/30'. They were both appreciated by the sensible Italians (every one an engineer and every engineer an artist, as northern Italians have been described) and A.L.F.A. prospered for a time. But despite the popularity of their cars A.L.F.A. fell into money troubles, to be rescued in 1915 by mining equipment manufacturer, Nicola Romeo.

Above The origins of this car go back to 1908 when as the SB4 it was seen at England's Brooklands track. The car was wrecked in 1921, and rebuilt in 1923 with an altered body and a new engine. It can still be seen in competition.

Below First of the Alfas, 1910, the 4·1 litre 20/30 Torpedo. Concurrently with this model the company produced a smaller 15/20 h.p. car.

Right By 1901 the Fiat organization was making its fourth production model (including a 6 h.p. racing car). This is an 8 h.p. with a front-mounted engine.

In 1924 Alfa Romeo entered driver Campari and their P2 racing car in their first Grand Prix—the French event at Lyon—and won handsomely. This 8-cylinder 2-litre supercharged car then dominated the last two years of the 2-litre Grand Prix Formula. The Type B 'Monoposto' (single-seater) appeared in 1932 (everybody called it the P3) and was one of the sport's first real single-seaters—the riding mechanic's seat had been done away with in 1925. With a powerful 190 b.h.p. at 5,400 r.p.m. developed by its 8-cylinder 2,653 c.c. unit, the P3 won the 1932 French, Italian, Monza and German Grands Prix, and the 2.3 Monza car scooped most of the other big events. In 1933 the company was nationalized and withdrew from racing.

Fiat, Lancia, Alfa Romeo; Italy's great historic marques are known to all. And there were others with a ring of quality about them, such as Isotta-Fraschini, a marque combining the names of two men who began by selling Renault cars in Italy as early as 1899. Not all that happy with their French products they began making their own cars, the first of which in 1902, was large, costly, and bore a close likeness to the current Mercedes. By 1919 they were making the famous straight-8, the '8' and '88', the cars beloved of the novelists of the period, who so often gave the Isotta to the book's villain and the Hispano-Suiza to the hero.

The Itala, made by Matteo Ceirano, was first seen in 1904, but it was the model of three years later that made the name memorable. In 1907 a French newspaper sponsored a fantastic race, from Peking to Paris, around 10,000 miles. An Itala won with Prince Borghese at the wheel after a near-incredible journey of 60 days.

It was Henry Ford who is credited with saying: 'Every time I see an Alfa Romeo pass by, I raise my hat.' He could have added a few more made in Italy, one of the four great motor manufacturing cornerstones of Europe . . . including an honourable mention of SPA, Bianchi, OM, Zust, Temperino and so on. . . .

Above Built in 1913 by coachbuilder Castagna for Count Marco Ricotti, this astonishing Alfa torpedo was used for several speed record attempts. It was one of the first road vehicles to use aerodynamic principles to improve speed performance.

Top right A 1914 Itala 50–70 h.p. from Matteo Ceirano, whose factory produced the first Fiats and whose one time book-keeper was Vincenzo Lancia. A small motoring world in those days . . .

Right 'Mamma Mia, she's beautiful!' The CA(Coppa delle Alpi) had a 37 h.p. engine and short wheelbase chassis, and was the liveliest of the 1929–32 range of Fiat 514s.

COMMERCIAL BREAK

Time: a Sunday morning in May. Place: somewhere on the London to Brighton road. The annual Brighton Run is under way. But this is not the famous one that everybody knows, which was the commemoration of the 'Emancipation Run' that in November 1896 first celebrated the Act of Parliament that freed the British motorist from the 4 m.p.h. speed limit. This Brighton Run is a more light-hearted affair, a rally of historic commercial vehicles over the same route. . . .

A steam bus and a 1920 Diesel road-sweeper vie with each other on the dual carriageway, their massive pistons beating a muffled drumbeat on the asphalt as they struggle along at 20 m.p.h. Small spidery Model T Ford vans of the 'twenties bob along the roads, their wooden artillery wheels making kaleidoscope colour-patterns in the sunshine.

A 1935 fire engine with a 100 ft. ladder, driven by three young enthusiasts, is seen chugging down the route. An enormous blue van with great brass headlights rams its way to Brighton—a McCurd, the only one left. A 1914 Foden steam wagon, all five tons of it, puffs asthmatically along, its chimney belching dark smoke. The day is counted successful if they just manage to arrive at Brighton, never mind the hour, and these old work-horses strain every piston—steam, petrol or diesel—to get to the coast that day. . . .

Above A Sentinel Super Platform lorry, vintage 1929, arrives at Brighton with steam to spare.

Below On the left, a 1933 steamer; struggling to keep up is a heavyweight Foden steam wagon built in 1914—and still running on wooden wheels.

Right 'Old Bill', a 1933 Sentinel steam timber haulage wagon raises steam before the start of the Commercial Brighton Run.

Left . . . Spidery Model T Ford vans bob along the Brighton Road . . . this one is a 1920 one-ton tipper, built in the U.S.A.

Left A towering McCurd, believed to be the only one extant, parked and docile in Brighton.

THE IRONWORKS AT VAUXHALL

Cromer 4 August 1903

Dear Sir,

You will be wondering how I got along with my Car. Well, she has acted like a charm all the way, and never refused duty at any time, taking the hills like level ground.

May I tell you that I took her across London bridge on Saturday morning, and drove through the Borough Market, where the traffic kept two policemen as busy as they could be. After that exploit I don't fear any traffic, although I still prefer the open country.

Yours faithfully, M. Smythe

Early customers like the writer of the above letter took it for granted that the Vauxhall Ironworks Company would be closely interested in their progress with the new vehicle, as indeed they were, in the leisurely turn-of-the-century days. And Vauxhall were proud of their product, first seen on the market the year this note was penned.

Below First of the line; the 1903 Vauxhall, made in the London works. Powered by a single-cylinder engine, horizontally mounted.

Top left Elegant and fast, the legendary Vauxhall 'Prince Henry'. The chassis price alone in 1911 was £485 and there were plenty of takers.

Above A Vauxhall 30/98, vintage 1927. Designed by Laurence Pomeroy in 1913 and so popular as a sporting or a touring vehicle that this model was produced until the late 'twenties.

Left '100 miles an hour on the track' was promised by its designer— and the promise was kept.

Scottish marine engineer Alexander Wilson had a background of designing and marketing which started long before the horseless carriage was dreamed of, and at the riverside factory he had designed and made steam engines for tugs, paddle steamers and other Thames traffic since 1857. However, business was disastrously poor towards the end of Victoria's reign, and the business was turned over to automobiles on the whim of the official receivers who were running the small factory—and who thought they would like to get in on the ground floor of the new transport industry.

The first Vauxhall was a light car. People took to its simplicity, its open body, its tiller steering and its low cost. At 130 guineas (front seat 6 gns extra) it introduced motoring to a wider public and its 40 m.p.g. helped to sustain their interest and participation. Two years later, so successful was the little Vauxhall, that Wilson brought out a more ambitious car, a 12/14 h.p. model with three cylinders and a steering wheel. Four years after opening for business, Vauxhall Motors Limited was formed to handle cars exclusively; by this time the factory had moved to the Hertfordshire town of Luton, famed then for its hats and hatters.

The story of the Vauxhall company has been studded with examples of bold, forward-thinking designs and products. Even in 1908, a bare six years after the first model, a Vauxhall easily won the R.A.C. and Scottish Reliability Trials, and a couple of years later a Vauxhall became the first 20 h.p. car to reach 100 m.p.h. That year also saw the prototype of the legendary Prince Henry

Vauxhall (named after Prince Henry of Prussia, whose deep interest in motor sport was well known), a sports tourer that achieved world renown. Flexible enough for family Sunday trips or thundering its way to victory at hill-climb events, the Prince Henry was one of the early motors that laid the foundation for modern sports car design. The first Prince Henry was a 4-cylinder 20 h.p. car selling for £485, but as its power and sophistication increased, its price by 1915 rose to £565.

The curiously named 30/98 (it was neither 30 h.p. nor 98 h.p. nor anything else that could be linked with those figures, and to this day no explanation of the title has been forthcoming) was an example of a tremendously successful car that was never intended as a production model. A derivative of the 1913 Prince Henry the 30/98

was made for competition purposes. It first appeared, with a full round radiator, at the Waddington Fells Hill Climb and made fastest-time-of-day. During World War I (only 13 were made before 1915 but they had already made a mark in the sport) it was modified further to be more easily constructed on regular production lines. Then in 1919, almost immediately after the war, it was made available to the public. Sporting enthusiasts queued to buy it at £1,350.

Top left 1906, and the first of the 'fluted' bonnets appear, a decorative feature that was to continue until 1959. This car was an experimental prototype with an 18 h.p. engine.
Above The start of Vauxhall's sporting successes. This 20 h.p. Vauxhall won the 1908 R.A.C. and Scottish Reliability Trials becoming the first car in the world to complete 2,000 miles without a single involuntary stop.

Right Grand old man of literature,
Bernard Shaw, at the wheel of his
Vauxhall 20/60, circa, 1927.

The 30/98 plunged into immediate success in motor sport. Its record between 1920 and 1923 alone stands at an astonishing 75 racing wins and 52 second places, and 14 hill-climb victories. And although Vauxhall fielded a works team, a high proportion of these successes were scored by private owners . . . already a far cry from the days a couple of decades earlier, when customers sent grateful thank-you notes to the company informing them that their Vauxhall managed to get from London to Leatherhead safely.

Below left Worth a frame of its own, as they used to say. The Vauxhall 30/98, one of the most successful sporting vehicles of the 'twenties. This is the 1913 model, then called the Vauxhall Velox Light Fast Tourer.

Below A Wensum boat-deck adds sportive distinction to this 30/98.

Vauxhall 30/98 (reprinted from catalogue) Fast, Light, Touring Car	
Engine:	Four cylinders 98 mm bore by 150 mm stroke, developing on the bench 100 b.h.p. R.A.C. rating 23.8 h.p. Cylinder capacity 4.5 litres.
Ignition:	High tension magneto, variable spark.
Clutch:	Vauxhall multi-disc.
Gearbox:	Four speeds and reverse. Direct on top.
Brakes:	Foot brake on propeller shaft; hand brake on rear axle hubs, diameter 12 inches.
Suspension:	Semi-elliptic springs, with Deri-hon shock absorbers throughout.
Petrol supply:	Tank at rear with air-pump pressure feed. Tank holds 12 gallons.
Body:	A special light body—the Vauxhall Velox—is built by the company.
Finish:	Nickel.

TIN LIZZIE

During the years of its production it trundled the length and breadth of the world. A sharp-edged black box, high-built to clear the rutted American roads, sedan or soft-topped, right or left drive, mild-mannered and mild-powered. The ubiquitous, immortal Model T Ford, the 'flivver', the 'Tin Lizzie', the 'ugly mule', butt of derisory jokes and limericks, the car that was simple, reliable, cheap (the original price of $850 in 1909 had reduced to $260 by 1925) and sold over 15 million between 1908 and 1927.

Henry Ford, the farm boy from Michigan who had gone up to the city to make good (although not quite so rustic and unlessoned as he is often made out to be) had run over halfway through the alphabet with his earlier models before producing the first truly universal car. Ford's backer wanted him to build big luxury cars. Although he disagreed with this policy he produced the 7-litre Model K, a car which sold poorly. Vindicated, Ford, started work on the Model T ('This car will have everything every customer wants', he said rashly) and

Below Henry Ford with his first attempt at an automobile. Its twin-cylinder power unit gave it 20 m.p.h. Ford made his second car two years later, in 1898.

his aim was that anyone who could ride a bicycle should be able to drive it.

The Model T had, by modern standards in Europe, a big engine, a 2,884 c.c. 4-cylinder unit which was cast as a single block with a removable cylinder head (at first) for ease of access to the pistons.

The car, built largely of vanadium steel, a new development giving much more strength than normal steel, weighed 13¾ cwt, had three foot pedals—right for braking, left for selecting the two forward speeds and neutral, and the middle one giving reverse. Beneath the steering wheel was a hand throttle, and the handbrake which as well as performing its usual function, operated the clutch. Petrol level was measured by dipping a rod or stick into the tank and checking depth (two inches equalled two gallons). It was also the first American car to have left-hand drive.

When Henry and a friend took the new Model T out on a test run in the autumn of 1907 they covered 1,357 miles (a marathon at the time) at 22 miles to the gallon.

The test confirmed that this was the car that could truly become the servant of the populace and the workhorse of commerce. And in the United States, a country wide open to development and free of the shackles of class and privilege, this was precisely what was needed. The car sold well—rather it sold astronomically well—more Model Ts were made than all other motor manufacturers' products put together during the years of its production. . . .

The ugly duckling T turned the motor industry upside down in more ways than one. After a few months of production Ford sent out a panic telegram to all his dealers: 'Do not send any more orders until advised by this office', he said. Ford turned his attention to faster ways of making the Model T—and mass-production on a large scale was born. Production almost doubled every year. Ford made 10,660 the first year of the Model T.

Below Heyday of the Model T. The touring version of 1915 was tough and had good ground clearance—prime requirements for travel on U.S. country roads.

In 1913, 168,220 left the factory; in 1923, two million were sold.

And Henry Ford was building new plants throughout the world. Moving assembly lines became more sophisticated, cutting production costs even more—and reducing dramatically the price to the customer. Henry Ford's brilliant application of moving belt assembly and synchronized production became the model upon which other industries were built.

The Germans coined the word 'Fordismus' meaning the mastery of mass-production, and author Aldous Huxley cast Ford in the role of the Almighty—and he was indeed a fair copy of a deity to many of his workers. They had been given a five-dollars-a-day rate by 1914—twice as much as the rest of the industry, and labour relations in the Ford company were far ahead of others. Henry Ford had always been the champion of the little man, and now, under the weight of a huge complex bringing vast profits, he did not change his character or his philosophy. . . .

A top speed of 40 m.p.h. was fine for early Model T Fords. Their ability to stand up to the pounding of unmetalled local roads, their versatility—they could be adapted for use on the farm or as light commercial vehicles or even, by jacking up the back and using one of the road wheels, as a lumber saw—endeared them to all, became a part of the American scene, and indeed changed radically the living habits of millions. You can still find them today, down on the farm in the more remote parts of the United States, used as circular saws, butter-making machines or personal transport. And the claim will hold good for some time, no doubt, for the Model T was designed to last more or less for ever.

Right Henderson, Texas, about 1923, when nearly every car was a Ford Model T.

STILL BEST IN THE WORLD

Take two men from as different backgrounds as could be found in the last century, bring them and their talents together—the talent for meticulous engineering, and a flair for selling—and the motor industry *could* have another Royce and Rolls.

The chances would be small, however. Royce for instance should have been a flour miller like his father in Peterborough. The family business was ailing when, at the age of 10, he found his first job—as a scarecrow! Later he sold newspapers, and in 1877 became a railway engineer.

That same year in Monmouthshire the wealthy Lord Llangattock was presented with a third son, the Hon. Charles Stewart Rolls. At the age of 14 when Charles went to Eton, Royce was then 28, and had branched out on his own on borrowed money into the electrical crane-building business.

Royce the crane-maker had a restless mind and, irritated by its unreliability, had taken his new French automobile to bits, learned its working principles—

and had built, by the spring of 1904, another, far more sophisticated one. Nine years previously, when Charles Rolls had been sent on a visit to France, he had been fascinated by the new $3\frac{3}{4}$ h.p. Peugeot. His background offered the usual late-Victorian occupations for the aristocracy, horses as a pastime, and as a career the army, the church or politics were expected of most younger sons. Young Charles would have none of them; he had already shown his probing, unconventional attitudes when, as a schoolboy, he had persuaded the family to let him install electric lights in the house, and was already a 'cad on casters'—a cyclist.

Charles Rolls bought the Peugeot and used it while he studied at Cambridge. He left with a degree in mechanics and applied science—and a great deal of driving experience. Shortly afterwards he won Britain's first motor sport event of any significance, the 1900 Thousand Miles Reliability Trial, in a 12 h.p. Panhard. In 1902 and 1903 he set up a new world land speed record in a Mors no less than three times. By 1904, with

partner Claude Johnson, Rolls had become the leading motor car distributor in England. One fact only disturbed him; there was not a single British car of sufficient quality for him to offer to the public.

Forty-one year-old Henry Royce had, in 1904, just completed his first car, one which had just a single point of similarity to the French car he had bought; a 2-cylinder 10 h.p. engine. The rest was pure Royce and far superior in engineering quality to anything ever made in Britain or France. On 1 April 1904, Henry Royce turned the starting handle and the car purred into life at the first pull, smooth and silent. Against this all other cars sounded like 'an avalanche of tea-trays' as a journalist remarked with bulls-eye accuracy. Said *The Times*: 'When the engine is running one can neither hear nor feel it, and pedestrians never seemed to hear the car's approach.'

Below The original Rolls-Royce Silver Ghost, a 40/50 h.p. 6-cylinder car, built in the early part of 1907. It is still in good running order after clocking up some half-a-million miles.

Rolls plus Royce

So the odds against their meeting became less astronomical. These two very different men had embarked on a similar venture—one selling cars and the other producing them. And each was searching for the perfect product. . . .

Henry Edmunds, a founder of the R.A.C. and often called the godfather of Rolls-Royce, brought the two men together, first by letter. Rolls suggested that Royce visit him in London. Royce was too busy. Eventually after some delicate negotiating Edmunds took Rolls to see the car. They met and talked in Manchester's Midland Hotel, and later tried out the 1.8 litre Royce car. It was too small for Rolls' taste, but he knew that he had met the one man in the country who could build to his exacting standards. Rolls agreed to sell Royce cars.

The name Rolls-Royce was minted at Christmas 1904, and in the spring of the next year Royce's second and third models came off the stocks at the Cooke Street Works in Manchester; a 3-cylinder 15 h.p. and a 4-cylinder 20 h.p. car. A 30 h.p. model was well on the way. In 1906 Rolls stopped selling other makes, and Rolls-Royce Limited was born.

In the autumn of 1906 the Motor Show at London exhibited the models of the day for the small group of people who could then afford to buy motor transport. Rolls-Royce had their new model on display—a car that marked the end of months of painstaking design. They called it the Silver Ghost.

The first appearance of the 40/50 h.p. Silver Ghost created wide interest. Well ahead of contemporary automobile engineering, it set new standards of operation and comfort, and the aristocratic were soon reluctant to be seen without one. Said *The Autocar*: 'There is no realization of driving propulsion; the feeling . . . is of being wafted through the landscape.' A Rolls-Royce still endows that wafting feeling. . . .

Below The Hon. Charles Rolls, aristocrat and adventurer. His restless mind moved on to aviation, and it was in the air he met his death, in 1910 at the age of 33.

Right Vintage Rolls-Royces line up for inspection at a motor pageant.

Below right The 15 h.p. 3-cylinder Rolls-Royce built during 1905/6.

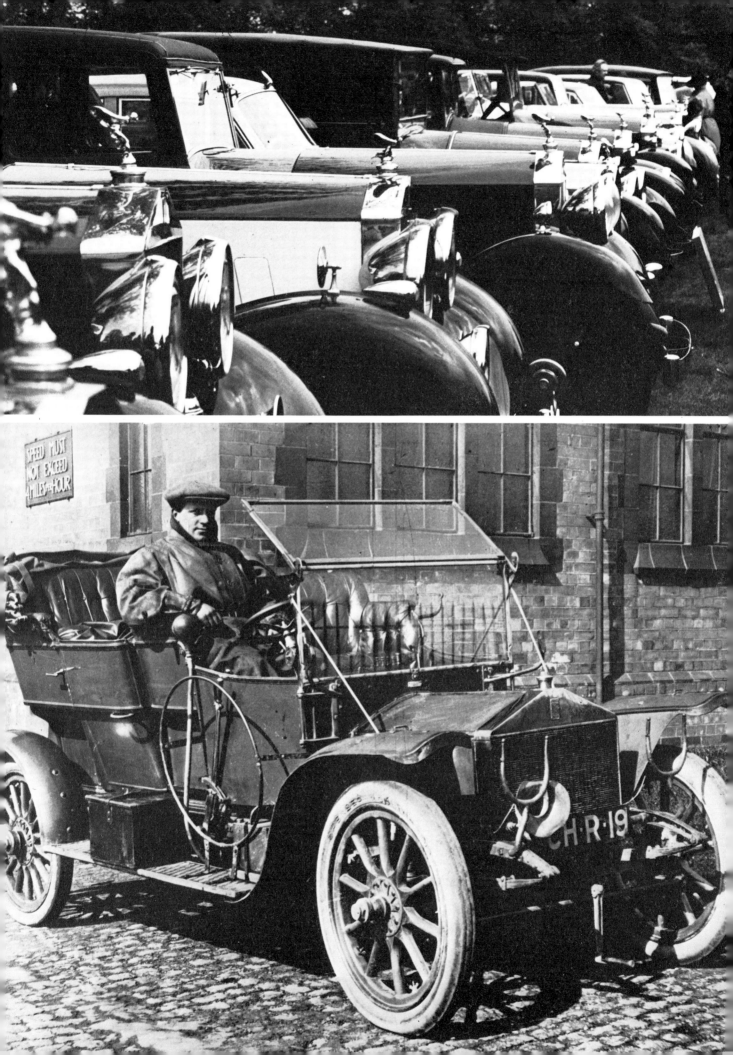

THE MOTORIST'S FRIEND

December 1897; a cold morning deteriorated into rain as a small group of men—almost all the automobilists in Britain—trooped into a large room near Whitehall, London, to form their own motoring society. They called it the Automobile Club of Great Britain and Ireland, the club which was ten years later to get His Majesty King Edward's assent to become the Royal Automobile Club.

The first task of the new organization was to make lists of ironmongers, chemists and blacksmiths, establishments that could provide the pioneer motorists with fuel, and undertake repairs. Its first secretary, C. S. Rolls' colleague Claude Johnson, was also the club's first public relations man and organized exhibitions, demonstrations, contests and rallies that would (hopefully) show the horseless carriage off to advantage. The first real breakthrough was the Thousand Miles Trial, the round-Britain rally which brought the motor car to the British public, or at least to those on the route, and when the Club mounted the 1902 Gordon Bennett race in Ireland—Britain's first international motor race— the R.A.C. became firmly entrenched as the national sporting body. It still is.

But life for the early twentieth century motorist was not all roses and open roads. The police, and equine-orientated justices of the peace brought down the full

Below In 1905 the infant Automobile Association enlisted cyclists who patrolled the Brighton and Portsmouth roads to pin-point police traps. Here, one of the earliest patrols escorts a motorist.

Below right The first A.A. experimental Channel crossing, 1908, with a 40 h.p. Crossley balanced precariously in the sling. This type of loading continued at several English Channel ports until well into the 1950s.

weight of their authority on the side of the horse. In 1904, the year the speed limit was raised to 20 m.p.h. heavy fines were imposed for the slightest motoring infringement, and hedgerow traps set up by the police punctuated country spins with expensive gambles.

Trapping in this way was naturally distasteful to the small and still exclusive motoring public. However, drivers could hardly object to the police enforcing the law. The spirit of sportsmanship diminished however, when the traps became even more frequent and on occasions somewhat suspect in their objectivity. An unofficial squad of bicycle scouts patrolled at least one main road, organized by racing driver Charles Jarrot and William Letts. These scouts warned drivers who were approaching speed traps, a system that teetered on the edge of illegality, but which gained great numbers of sympathizers. In 1905 the small group formed itself into the Automobile Mutual Association, dropping the 'Mutual' soon afterwards.

The A.A. appealed for recruits and appointed a secretary, Stenson Cooke, who got the job mainly because he owed a small sum of money to a friend who happened to be acting as the Association's temporary unpaid legal adviser. The A.A. has many reasons to be thankful to Cooke's financial embarrassment that day.

The A.A. was more militant than the R.A.C. which

in fact had been founded as a 'focus for enthusiasts' having something of a social flavour, and had assumed the guardianship of motor sport in Britain, rather than the mantle of protector against the outrageous fortunes of early motoring. The Automobile Association's prime concern was the protection of members against what they considered had changed from prosecution to persecution. Members who were saved from a trap often sent in a grateful guinea to the A.A. The defence of members summoned to court for motoring offences began when one member was stopped by police who accused him of speeding, though a nearby A.A. scout confirmed that he had been doing no more than 15 m.p.h. Police evidence was believed and the motorist fined £5. The poor patrolman was thrown into Brixton Prison for perjury. The A.A. decided to appeal. They won, and provided legal counsel for members.

The early years of patrols and the 20 m.p.h. limit encouraged the lack of communication between the A.A. and the police, but the breach was slowly healed as patrolmen co-operated more and more with the police in work connected with motoring—point-duties, first-aid work, helping stranded motorists. Collaboration between the police and the two motoring organizations grew to close co-operation as they began to complement each other's role.

In the Metropolitan Police District.

To *Walter C Bersey*

of *39 Victoria Street, Westminster*

INFORMATION ———————————— has been *laid*

this day by *George Dixon*

for that you, on the *20th* Day of *October*

in the Year One Thousand Eight Hundred and Ninety *six*

at — *Parliament Street*

within the District aforesaid, did *unlawfully drive a certain locomotive, to wit; a motor car, through a certain town at a greater speed than two miles an hour.*

ad. 1865.

Contrary to the Statute etc

YOU ARE THEREFORE hereby summoned to appear before the Court of Summary Jurisdiction, sitting at the *Bow Street* Police Court on *Satur* day the *31st* day of *October 1896* at the hour of *two* in the *after* noon, to answer to the said *information*.

Dated the *23rd* day of *October*

One Thousand Eight Hundred and Ninety *six*

F Lushington

One of the Magistrates of the Police Courts of the Metropolis.

SCH. I.—2.

SUMMONS.

GENERAL FORM SUMMARY
CASES.

S. J. A. Rules, 1886—2.

W B & L (484υ)—64151—10000-6-96

Above, left and right Issued just before the 'Emancipation Act', two summonses requiring a motorist to appear in Court in Bow Street for exceeding the 2 m.p.h. town limit, and for neglecting to be preceded by a footman.

In the Metropolitan Police District.

To *Walter C Bersey*

of *39 Victoria Street, Westminster*

INFORMATION ─────────────────── has been *laid*

this day by *George Dixon*

for that you, on the *20th* Day of *October*

in the Year One Thousand Eight Hundred and Ninety *six*

at *a certain public highway, to wit Parliament Street*

within the District aforesaid, ~~did~~ *being the owner and having the charge of a locomotive propelled by other than animal power, to wit, a motor car, did unlawfully neglect to have such locomotive whilst in motion preceded by at least 20 yards by a person on foot*

Contrary to the Statute etc

YOU ARE THEREFORE hereby summoned to appear before the Court of Summary Jurisdiction, sitting at the *Bow Street* Police Court on *Satur* day the *31st* day of *October* at the hour of *two* in the *after* noon, to answer to the said *information*.

Dated the *23d* day of *October*

One Thousand Eight Hundred and Ninety *six*

H Lushington

One of the Magistrates of the Police Courts of the Metropolis.

PROHIBITION AND THE DUESENBERG

Let us dispense with the astonishing statistics first: American passenger car production in 1905 was 24,250; in 1910 the figure was 181,000; in 1915, 895,930 cars were made, and by 1917, the year of that country's tardy but powerful entry into the Great War, the figure was 1,745,792. With its infinite raw material resources, its almost limitless manpower, and its (by 1917) highly sophisticated production systems, America could afford to continue making private cars through the war years, and production dropped to less than a million only in 1918. By 1920 production was again the highest-ever with 1,905,560 automobiles.

The American automobile industry before World War I was a shifting sea of mergers, amalgamations, movements of a small number of brilliant top men from one ailing company to another, (usually with the subsequent rise of that company) group and corporation formations.

One of the new and hopeful manufacturing companies of this period was Dodge. John and Henry Dodge had worked for Ford, building engines in their own workshops. In 1913 the Dodge brothers, realizing that their entire business was dependent upon Ford orders, and having no assurance that the orders would continue indefinitely, withdrew their services as contributors to Ford manufacture. Then they sued Ford for the dividends of their substantial holdings, and collected $19 million. Quite enough to start the Dodge Company in 1914, even without the $27 million Henry gave them for the shares themselves.

The Dodge Company well illustrates the U.S. industry's movement and fortunes through the two decades after World War I. Their cars from the outset were designed as dependable 'with constant improvement but no yearly model change', virtues not calculated to hit the headlines, but nevertheless ones with their own solid values. During the war the workaday Dodge had doubled as ambulance and staff car, which did the company no harm at all and by 1920 it was in second place in the U.S. production race.

Dodge to Chrysler

The company had a big year when the Dodge all-steel closed sedan first appeared in 1923, an American first. The 4-cylinder cars were, like most other U.S. manufacturers' medium-size cars, very much the same in concept from 1915 through to 1927. Then in 1928 a low-priced 6-cylinder car was shown; with a capacity of 208 cu. ins. it developed 58 b.h.p. at 3,000 r.p.m. and sold at a popular $765. By which time the American business game of musical chairs had shunted the Dodge company to Walter Chrysler for $175 million.

Undoubtedly, the 1929 Senior Six Series S was the most luxurious car made by Dodge up to that year. With a 224 cu. ins. L-head engine on a seven-bearing crank shaft, big tyres, Stromberg UX-3 carburation, wire wheels and various sports-bodied alternatives, the car was compared to the Marmon 68 of the same season. A real metamorphosis for a plain car company with a 1914 model just a little above the Model T Ford.

The ordinary motorist in the States in the early 'twenties was likely to be a farmer, a mobile professional such as a doctor or a commercial traveller, or a middle-class pioneer commuter. Roads in the early 'twenties were still uncertain if not unconquerable, signposts were still something to guide a Wells Fargo coach and roadside facilities, in all but major strategic positions, were genuine backwoods vignettes. But to be fair, by the time the dust of war had settled the authorities had begun to notice that the automobile was here to stay and that there would only too soon be some very knotty problems connected with increasing numbers and increasing speeds. At this time (at 12.01 a.m. on 17 January 1920 to be precise) there came into force the 18th Amendment of the Constitution of the United States—the Prohibition Act. It heralded in the era of the getaway car, the fast town driver, the two-wheel cornering technique, and a host of rather special constructional developments. . . .

During the same eventful year the first Duesenberg appeared. For some years Fred Duesenberg had made cars that had won their laurels in the racing field; now the public were to be able to sample them. And a great privilege it was—the cars probably represented the zenith of U.S. quality production. With a 4.5. in-line 8-cylinder unit developing 100 b.h.p. the Model A was both racy and luxurious, a combination always difficult to produce. Needless to say film stars and mobsters loved it—and the Straight-8 Packards, the V-8 Cadillacs and Lincolns of the day.

Broadsides on Main Street

When two rival gangs met in their armoured vehicles, the ensuing battle could be like that of eighteenth century ships-of-the-line, each firing massive broadsides at the other when passing flank to flank. The naval simile continued with the fact that the gangs would use small fleets of men o'war in their street engagements. In one such battle at Cicero, Illinois, 10 cars at 12-foot intervals steamed, like capital ships at Trafalgar, down the main street and as each passed the restaurant in which Capone was assumed to be dining, it blazed off a fusillade into the windows. Most of these cars were in the fashion of the day, side-screened touring cars with canvas roofs. Tourers, with their mica windows, allowed a wider arc of fire than pillared sedans.

Some of these gangland cars of the 'twenties had remarkable modifications. Gun ports in the windscreen were not unknown; petrol tanks sheathed in steel, thick metal plate around the coachwork to window level, and in the odd sedan, a wind-down rear window for a stern salvo. Beautiful stuff, if a trifle heavy. And so dignified under a load of funeral flowers. . . .

General Motors had been in existence for 15 years when Walter P. Chrysler took over the Maxwell Motor Corporation after working for both Buick and G.M. On 5 January 1924 the first car to bear his name, a high-compression 6-cylinder 3½-litre with 7-bearing crankshaft, with air cleaner, replaceable oil filter and four-wheel hydraulic brakes (sensational development at that date) was offered to the public. Immediate acceptance was the reward of painstaking design, and Chrysler—the Corporation was formed in 1925—went on to produce the '70' '72' '75' and '77' and by 1931 the Deluxe Eight, Chrysler's first 8-cylinder model. This one cost $1,565, had free-wheeling (a dubious advantage) and another new sales feature, automatic spark control.

The early part of this decade was one of extremely rapid development for the automotive industry in the United States. With mass production now in full flow the numbers of cars manufactured yearly leapt from two million to nearly four million, although due to

Below Street scene in Detroit, 1920. America built private vehicles right through World War I, and by the date of this picture had hit its highest-ever annual production figure with 1,905,560 cars.

increasing standardization the choice of vehicle style, size and quality, was more limited. But Chrysler deliberately aimed at variety and in 1926 introduced the Imperial '80', a high-speed luxury car; in effect a new marque, designed to invade the luxury market.

The day Chrysler bought the Dodge Company the Corporation became one of the three great motor industries of the United States, ranking with Ford and General Motors. Chrysler then continued to pursue the policy of variety for the middle-market in an attempt to blanket the differing requirements, and in 1928 launched his own brainchild, the Plymouth . . . 'an absolutely new development in motor car style. New slender profile chromium-plated radiator . . . long low bodies . . . generous room for 2 to 5 passengers . . . new Silver Dome high compression engine, for use with any gasoline . . . smooth speed up to 60 and more miles an hour . . .' and so on, as the promotional eulogies proclaimed. It sold 58,000 in its first year of production.

A couple of months previously another Chrysler product, the slightly more expensive De Soto had come off the line for the first time. A two-seater of 3.2 litres (174.9 cu. ins.) this was also part of Chrysler's complex diversification plan and was aimed at hiving some of the sales away from Oldsmobiles and other medium-priced competitors.

And of course the Model T Ford was ubiquitous in the 'twenties. The go-anywhere car with its high ground clearance and big wheels was ideally suited to the early 'twenties when roads still demanded a large gap between their surface and the works of a car. In 1927 by which time 15 million Model Ts had been made, roads had begun to get straight and level in most places—most places between big towns that is; for some decades to come many minor American roads stayed as they were in coach-and-horses time. Later, in the years of the depression, the authorities used the unhappy state of mass unemployment to start building a great network of highways across the country, and began to study the ever-growing problems of parking, throughway traffic flows, rush-hour travel and other insoluble problems that beset today's motoring.

Day of the Duesenberg

'The best, the fastest, the longest-lasting car of our time', was the somewhat clumsy way the admen introduced in 1921 a car that really was all those things and more.

Thirty-year old salesman-racing driver, Erret Lobban Cord, had taken charge of the Auburn and Duesenberg companies in 1924, eschewing the mass market in favour of quality. He re-jigged both companies and produced, through Auburn, a series of 4-, 6- and 8-cylinder cars, and by 1928 had made the Model J Duesenberg a reality. Fred Duesenberg's new car was indeed something to boast about. Best, faster and long-lasting as the ads said, it had 6.9-litre twin-overhead-camshaft 8-cylinder motor, a top speed of round 116 m.p.h., and a chassis-only price of $8,500 (sky-high when compared with any other U.S. product, and more than the current Rolls-Royce). Delighted Americans with long purses bought the sleek, low vehicle at finished prices of up to $18,000, and it proved so popular with Gary Cooper, Mae West, Clark Gable *et al*, that in 1932 Duesenberg brought out his truly amazing 'SJ', with no less than 320 b.h.p. under the hood, a maximum speed *in second gear* of 104 m.p.h. and 129 in top! The few European monarchs who could afford the price bought one but the majority could be seen fender-to-fender at Hollywood's MGM studios. The name died in 1937, when the Cord organization fell—but several Duesenbergs remain as monuments to the finest technical achievement of immigrant Fred Duesenberg.

Below Classic American; a Series K Stutz touring car of 1922. Early rivalry between this marque and Mercer, the other popular U.S. sporting breed, had been fiercest before the First War.

Top right A 1929 Packard, preserved for posterity and seen here during a *concours d'élégance* at Britain's Oulton Park circuit.

Right The great Duesenberg Model J, 1929, with a 6·9 litre twin-overhead-camshaft power unit of 8 cylinders, this astonishing product could cost anything up to $18,000.

TREKKING OVER AFRICA... AND OTHER PLACES

Since motoring began and competition had caught the imagination, since the early rapid development of bigger and faster vehicles, since the organizing of longer and more hair-raising races, there had been a small coterie of motorists who had thrived on the razor-edge excitements of the new sport in a more swash-buckling way than most.

And when the blood-letting of the last capital-to-capital race had proved to be the catalyst that changed the form of the sport to closed circuit racing, this small clique needed more than a quick whirl round the Targo Florio circuit to keep them happy. They dreamed up impossibly difficult races, marathons over deserts and mountains, events designed to test men and cars to destruction or to promote them to lasting fame. Later, these long-distance feats—overland treks rather than competitions—were mounted to publicize the virtues of various marques, and were incredibly formidable.

Peking to Paris

A German, Dr. Lehwess, had started it all in 1902 when he set out in his Panhard, a car he called *Passe Partout*, after Jules Verne's character from *Round the World in 80 Days*, to drive eastwards from London, through

Russia, over the Pacific to San Francisco and New York and take ship back to Britain. His car ran well, but the roads—when there were any—proved beyond remedy. His attempt ended when his car disappeared in a snow-drift near St. Petersburg. However, others followed his example. An Englishman started out from Coventry for Turkey in an 8 h.p. Rover in 1905. East of the Danube roads shrank into tracks, his Rover became an object of awe and petrol had never been heard of. Nevertheless R. L. Jefferson and his Rover arrived at the Turkish capital in good order, the first motorist to cross the Balkan States.

Then in 1907 the French Newspaper *Le Matin* organized a race of 10,000 miles, from Peking in China to Paris, over completely unknown roads for most of the way. The competing cars were a 40 h.p. Itala, a small Spyker from Holland, two de Dion-Boutons, smaller still at 10 h.p. each, and a Contal tri-car of minute proportions.

The Itala, driven by the Italian Prince Borghese, took up the lead immediately the five-strong field passed through Peking's Gate of Virtue Triumphant. Using a number of devices to negotiate the dozens of different hazards on the route (it carried its own rails to cross broken bridges for instance) the Itala forged ahead, followed by the Spyker, the De Dions and the Contal, for which the others would wait every few hours.

Chinese peasants were pressed into service drawing the cars through flooded fields and hauling them, in the manner of ancient cannon, up steep mountainsides. For some of the way the cars used the bed of the Trans-Siberian Railway as their route—it was the only road available in that part of Russia—and here one of the Itala's wheels shed its spokes. Borghese took the wheel first to a public baths, hoping to swell the wood back into place, then, more sensibly, to a Siberian blacksmith, who did the job well. Warsaw was reached by the leading car, then, on genuine roads again, the Itala cruised into Paris just 60 days after starting from Peking. The rest arrived three weeks later.

As a race, the Peking-to-Paris event was an expensive joke. But in fact racing was not the prime object of the

Below left Peking to Paris, 1907. The Itala takes to the Trans-Siberian Railway for part of the 10,000 mile route . . .

Below . . . and is hauled across a broken bridge at a later stage of the 'race', looking here as though its days on the road under its own power are over. The Itala won the event, however.

exercise, which was to introduce the motor car and its virtues to far-flung parts of the world. This it did, allaying, eventually, the suspicions of the Chinese government that the event was either a practice invasion of their country or an attempt to imply that their railways were less efficient than motor transport.

The race also stimulated greater interest in world-girdling events, and another even more ambitious race was set up the following year, this time a slog from New York, over the Bering Straits to Asia and covering some of the previous year's route, finishing up at Paris; an almost-round-the-world race.

A February start ensured that within 20 miles of the line-up the cars were being dug out of snowdrifts, and that the Bering Straits were unapproachable from either side. The route was diverted to Yokohama by ship, thence by another ship to Vladivostock and onwards. Pot-shots by bandits and arrest for espionage were just two of the incidental troubles that were not directly attributable to the petrol engine.

An American, Thomas Flyer, won the race although a German Protos arrived first in Paris. It was placed second as it had travelled over part of the American section by train. So, by this Marco Polo-type event in the first decade of the twentieth century motoring was taken to the faraway places of the world and slowly, painfully, the age of motoring spread to the Orient. . . .

Conquest of Africa

Although they were commercially slanted, the African and Asian exploits of the French companies of Renault and Citroën in the 'twenties are no less part of motoring history. They helped to prove that the car of that time could be tough and reliable, that a determined and dedicated driver could conduct his vehicle where previously only missionaries had endeavoured to bring

Below Mountain crossing—the hard way. A Fiat takes a somewhat minor road over the Alps in 1924.
Right A Renault 'Routier du Désert' 13-h.p. six-wheeler (four of them were driven wheels) of the type that opened up a regular route across the Sahara in 1923.
Below right Citroën's Black Cruise 1925. A B2 fords a river near Lake Nyasa.

the doubtful benefits of the twentieth century to the dark continent.

Citroën seem to have started it. In December 1922 a Citroën half-track travelled from Touggourt to Timbuctoo, crossing the Sahara Desert for the first time in a motor vehicle. The President of France, no less, then suggested to André Citroën that his company could render a service to the country by proving that Madagascar, off the east coast of Africa and a French possession, was not as isolated as geographers implied, and how useful it would be to demonstrate that road communication between France, Africa and the great island of Madagascar was a feasible proposition.

André Citroën took a full year to prepare the Black Cruise, as it was called. Led by Georges-Marie Haardt, the expedition drove in eight half-tracks an agonizing 12,500 miles from Morocco through the very centre of Africa, the Congo, striking east and south to Mozambique. It was a massive safari, requiring five auxilliary expeditions to provide food, fuel, spares, and to relay films and records back to base. Through savannah, swamp, forest, parts of the route were covered by guess-work, having no recognizable landmarks for stretches of up to five hundred miles. River crossings were made on log rafts; paths hacked by hand out of the jungle were the normal highways over parts of the route, and five miles a day was the average through the densest vegetation. The convoy reached Madagascar on 20 June 1925, having blazed most of its trail for the first time. It gave more new information to natural science than it helped create a new way of getting to Madagascar.

Meanwhile Louis Renault, not to be outflanked by his arch-rival, André Citroën, had set up his own excursion into the desert. His 13 h.p. six-wheelers opened up the territory, which included the Sahara, that lure of French motor manufacturers, between the end of the Algerian railway and the railhead at the Niger. They took just seven days to cover the 1,500 miles of torrid heat and freezing nights. Thereafter the French considered the Sahara Desert a bus-route and used it as such.

All that remained, said Renault, was to drive down the length of Africa. But not in the grand manner of the Citroën procession. This trip should be done in a more domestic way. A husband-and-wife team would capture the interest of the press, and set Citroën by the ears, would it not? And in a single 13.9 h.p. Renault, Commandant Delingette, his wife and a mechanic started out for Capetown on 15 November 1925, arriving seven months later after the now usual gymnastics over river, swamp, jungle, mud and mountain. Thus the first solo crossing of Africa by car.

Previous page Crossing the foothills of the Himalayas in 1931 through deep snow and ice-covered rivers—and hot sun by the look of the pith helmets. Citroën's Croisière Jaune.

Right The Croisière Jaune, the Citroën saga via the Himalayas and the Gobi Desert. Here one of the half-tracks is suspended in mid-air after the mountain roads have crumbled beneath it.

The two French motor manufacturers had by now been severely bitten by trans-African motormania and sent clutches of cars all over the place, taking much of the publicity impact out of the undoubtedly historic feats. But the 1927 trip of Lieutenant George Estienne, hero of the earlier Renault expedition, is noteworthy. He was given the job of crossing the Sahara in a small touring car—a standard 8.3 h.p. torpedo at that.

He was officially commissioned to find new routes between several railheads and with a few cans of oil set off southwards from Algeria. Driving alone under the brazen sun of the desert, knowing that if anything went wrong with his undistinguished little vehicle he would have a dangerously long wait for one of the heavies using the route, he pressed on—to create a new speed record for the crossing to Gao on the River Niger in Mali. Estienne went on, doubling back and forth, checking routes, until he had covered 11,000 miles in 36 days, without even changing a sparking plug. His lonely exploit gave a tremendous sales boost to the little Renault car.

Four years later, in April 1931, Citroën set up the one to end them all, *La Croisière Jaune*, the Yellow Cruise. This was a 40-man, 14-half-track venture across Asia from the Mediterranean to Peking—the reverse of the route taken by those effervescent motor sport pioneers in 1907, but spiced with more difficult terrain across the Himalayas and over the Gobi Desert, the old 'silk route' of Marco Polo. The distance was 7,527 miles and the fun encompassed an Afghanistan revolution and a Chinese war. The expedition had split up into two groups, starting from each end of the line, with plans to meet in the middle, north of Tibet.

Irritants such as a temperature of 122°F. in the shade, a 500 mile detour and narrow mule tracks over the mountains with passes up to 13,000 ft., were accepted and overcome. Driving at 3 m.p.h., scraping the vertical inner surface of the cliff, with a dizzying drop to the other side, one of the car's crew was faced with their road crumbling away beneath them. They rebuilt the stone track with the vehicle suspended in mid-air. On other occasions the mountain tracks were actually three or four inches *narrower* than the half-tracks: the crews, said one report with some understatement, took those parts more carefully.

It is not quite certain if the object of this expedition was to open another commercial route or to prove that China was nearer than one thought if one travelled by Citroën, but it certainly drew attention to the ruggedness of the vehicles, and the courage of their crews. . . .

These motoring expeditions may not have been quite so academic as those, for instance, to the North and South Poles. Their purpose was basically commercial; but in the 'twenties and 'thirties men had not conquered all there was to conquer in the motor car. The challenge, like the age-old mountain-challenge, was still there. And, as usual, there were the men who could not resist taking up such a gauntlet. . . .

CARRIAGE TO CAR

It was well after the end of World War II before many car body designs shed the last vestiges of their carriage ancestors. Tucked-in-at-the-bottom door shapes of early private vehicles was a direct influence of the small-floor carriages of the previous century, and with a few notable exceptions designers paid at least subconscious homage to the car's horse-drawn forbears, with its welled body deep-slung between large wheels. Nobody had quite known where to locate the machinery when the car first appeared. Benz and Daimler put it at the car's rear end. Levassor first put it amidships, un-comfortably adjacent to passenger's rear ends, then brought it forward 'nearest the accident' where it stayed.

This early game of musical chairs with the powerpack gave rise to all sorts of bodywork gymnastics, with seats facing every whichway, and mostly adapted from the horse age. There were a few which had drivers *and* passengers facing forwards, although many pictures of them indicate that they were petrified of falling into the space where the horse used to be. . . .

Right One can almost see the horse in the shafts in this picture of an 1894 Benz Viktoria. Yet Benz considered that he built his early vehicles with little reference to the horse-drawn carriage.

Right Benz called it a Landaulet-Coupé. A Landaulet because the rear portion of the roof could be let down, and a coupé as the car is literally 'cut' between the closed passenger area and the exposed driver's seat.

Straight out of the carriage showroom, this 1899 model was more conventional than most of Benz' vehicles of that date.

Left This 1907 Laurin-Klement taxi from Bohemia had shed much of the early horse-and-coach design influence. L & K used much of their previous motor cycle expertise to produce several fine models. This company was taken over in 1925 by the arms firm of Skoda.

Below The year is 1920, and the torpedo (open tourer) with its unbroken line from front to rear, or at least as far as the windscreen, is in fashion with the open-air set.

Veteran Coachwork Terms

The terms used for the design of the first motor vehicles were as one would expect, taken from the horse-drawn world. Phaetons, dog-carts, victorias, landaus and so on came straight out of the Victorian age into the twentieth century un-changed—except for the absence of the nag-at-the-front—and it took a few years for motor cars to be different enough to earn names of their own.

There was much confusion at the beginning and terms that meant one shape to a European meant something quite different to an American—who in any case had a set of his own not used in Europe—sedan, buckboard, buggy, roadster and others—and some of the terms have never made complete sense to anyone. However, a few basic ones were widely used. . . .

Vis-à-Vis: literally, face-to-face. Passengers (and driver) sat facing each other usually in pairs.

Dos-à-Dos: the reverse of a vis-à-vis, or back-to-back.

Landau: taken from the name of the German town, this vehicle had a collapsible roof for the rear passengers to obtain a better view of passing interests. A laundaulette was a smaller form of landau.

Tonneau: An open car with the rear seats curved to allow a central rear door.

Phaeton: a light car with seats for two and the minimum of coachwork, similar to an early racing car. Phaetons could be double (four seats) triple, or closed. Sometimes also called a spider, or spyder.

Voiturette: like a phaeton this had two seats and was usually an open light vehicle.

Berlina: a saloon, usually in the luxury category.

Coupé: the earliest coupé limousines had divisions between passengers and chauffeur—literally 'cut' down the middle. The driver was exposed to the elements under an open roof, but the passenger compartment was closed.

Brake: originally a light vehicle with which horses were broken to harness, a brake (or break) in motoring terms, was a family (or shooting party) wagon-type car often with 'tram' seats at the rear.

Torpedo: continental term for an open four-seater tourer with soft hood and sporting tendencies, and in which the line of the bonnet was continued back to the rear of the car.

Viktoria: driving seats up front (usually before engines were located there) and a deep luxury double-seat at the rear protected by a large pram-type hood.

Above A 1909 Riley on manoeuvres. Long gone are the extravagances and design vagaries of the late 19th century and the motor car has acquired a form of its own, with only vestigial equine influences.

GAS TO GASOLINE

. . . or petrol, essence, benzina, dependent on where you live. From petra meaning a rock, and oleum, a form of oil, comes the word petroleum—rock or mineral oil. Or, rather, crude oil; because the stuff that drives internal combustion engines is a long way from the raw product. It has a remarkable quality of being found where it is not needed, and hardly ever where it is, and it is almost always found in a state in which it cannot be used, necessitating complex processing before yielding its range of fuels, oils, solids and so on. It has been around a few million years; it has been known for 5,000 years. It may just last another 50 at the present rate of consumption.

A solid form of petroleum bitumen-asphalt was used by Abraham's children to mortar their bricks: mosaics of bitumen have been found at Ur, the oldest city in the world and the cradle, it is said, of civilization. Bitumen, mineral pitch, was used to 'pitch-caulk' Noah's Ark, under reputedly direct instructions from the Almighty, and many of the 'eternal fires' of history and folk lore have been crude oil surfacing and set alight by nature or accident, to say nothing of the countless miracles of

'burning waters' etc., emanating from the same scource.

And boring for oil is no modern innovation. The Caliph of Baghdad leased a concession to a commercial tycoon called Darband in AD 885, and mineral oils were exported in Marco Polo's day. . . . Then on 27 August 1859 one Edwin Drake struck Pennsylvania oil at 69 feet. And even he was only searching for something better than whale-oil for use in lamps. The automobile was still 26 years away. . . .

An internal 'explosion' engine had been developed in the late eighteenth century by a Swiss, De Rivaz, using coal gas, and an Englishman Robert Street had worked on the same lines. Later gas motors were the genuine ancestors of the internal combustion engine as we know it today, pioneered by Lenoir, who is recognized as the first man to make a practical 'town' gas engine. Nikolaus Otto, a Cologne merchant, went a step farther and in 1867 he and his partner Langen showed an atmospheric (without compression) gas engine—and were awarded first prize in the Paris World Exhibition for the most efficient engine. Otto went on to design the four-stroke engine. Some years earlier,

however, the British chemist Michael Faraday had discovered that benzene was present in coal-tar and could be used as a fuel in liquid form.

Otto's later engine was powered by liquid fuel. He had requested a patent for the use of a 'mixture of gas ignited by spark' and explained that 'this does not mean a combination of gas and air, but of the vapour emanating from a hydro-carbon liquid', benzene or petrol.

Then in 1875 after several attempts to adapt their gas engines to operate on petroleum distillates, the directors of the Gasmotoren-Fabrik Deutz gave their factory manager, Gottlieb Daimler, a directive to develop a 'petroleum engine', one which had the advantage of independence from a piped and fixed local gas supply. So the modern petrol engine was born, curiously enough against Daimler's wishes. He was at the time still in favour of continuing to produce the atmospheric engine. . . .

Below left Pioneer days in the oil world. Drilling in the Niger Delta by the British Colonial Petroleum Company in 1910.

Below Remember the hand-operated petrol pump? A filling station of the 'twenties in Switzerland.

TOP BRASS

One of the delights of visiting a veteran meeting is the aura of the fashionable turn-of-the-century, especially if the gathering is held in the grounds of one of the more stately houses of the country. Vignettes of the past are everywhere—the vehicles themselves, tall and dignified, burnished relics of a bygone age kept alive and vibrant by the dedication of their owners. Small gems abound— a can of 'Pioneer Spirit' fixed on a running board, a high horizontal wooden steering wheel or an acetylene lamp as big as a stewpan, the startling colour of an artillery wheel, and the brasswork reflecting your own face as you admire the solid worth of such cars. . . .

Left W. R. Morris launched his Morris Oxford in 1913. With two seats and an 8·9 h.p. White and Poppe engine, it laid the foundation for the company's later success.

Below *Get out of the way or I'll bite you.* The loud end of a serpent-horn of the Edwardian period.

Bottom The sparkling 4-litre T-head engine of a 1909 Humber.

Right Warning glory—in the shape of a horn and lamps—of a 1909 Renault.

Bottom right The bold brass front of a 1909 Star.

Above Leather-and-brass Edwardiana. This 1904 Peugeot swing-seat tonneau with its 2-cylinder 9 h.p. unit, 3 speed box and cone clutch, was sophisticated for its year.

VINCENZO LANCIA

The bicycle manufacturing company of Ceirano had moved with the times and turned to automobiles under the direction of a group of financiers that were soon to become known as the F.I.A.T. organization. In 1898 the company took on a new book-keeper, 17 year-old Vincenzo, son of the landlord of the Ceirano premises and maker of soups, Giuseppe Lancia.

Young Lancia however was not exactly captivated by double-entry book-keeping, but was fascinated by the company's engineering section. He soon began to concern himself with engineering problems and such was his flair for the subject that he quickly acquired a reputation for an insight into complex repair and mechanical problems. By 1900—before he was 20 years old—he was chief inspector of the factory, now under Fiat direction.

The early Fiat policy of sales promotion through racing successes took Vincenzo Lancia to sporting fame in one of Fiat's first races, at Padua, where he won at the wheel of a 6 h.p. car. Lancia rapidly acquired a high reputation in motor racing. His skilful, courageous and cool driving technique was designed to get the absolute maximum from his car, without pushing the machine beyond its capabilities—a technique used widely 60

Above Vincenzo Lancia at the tall wheel of the 110 h.p. Fiat that took part in the 1905 (the last) Gordon Bennett race, held at Clermont-Ferrand in France.

years later, but one that was not in many competition drivers' repertoires in the thrills-and-spills days of the infant sport.

Thereafter Lancia drove in many of the early epic races; the 1903 Paris-Madrid event, the Coppa Florio, the Gordon Bennett and the Vanderbilt Cup races. Then in 1906 he formed his own company.

The first Lancia, built in a small works in Turin, appeared on the road in September 1907 (after Lancia and his workers had widened the factory's main door with a pick-axe to let it out) following a delay caused by a stove fire which destroyed a numer of original drawings and patterns.

This first car was no mere Fiat copy. Some of its fundamental principles went directly against the current technical trends. Lancia had built a light, low chassis with a shaft drive, and a 4-cylinder 2,543 c.c. side-valve engine developing 14 h.p. at 1,450 r.p.m. Shaft drive had been pioneered by Louis Renault but most cars still used chain drive in 1906; also at this date engine speeds rarely exceeded 1,000 r.p.m.—this unit could reach

1,800 r.p.m. Lancia's No. 1, called Alpha (the Greek alphabet was used to designate different Lancia types for over 20 years) had moved sharply away from tradition, and of course was heavily criticized for its light weight, its high engine speed, and its 'perilous' top speed of 56 m.p.h.

Although Vincenzo Lancia was not interested in racing his own vehicles, Lancia production cars scored a number of firsts in private hands during the first years of the marque's life. By 1913 the Theta offered built-in electrics for the first time in Europe. Lancia's 12-cylinder overhead camshaft engine was in production by 1919—although this highly sophisticated engine proved uneconomical to produce.

Then in 1922 came Lancia's greatest offering, the Lambda, the result of several years of design effort. Having seen and analysed the behaviour of a ship on which he was travelling in heavy seas, Lancia adapted the principle of monocoque, or unitary, construction to his car. One of his engineers wrote at the time: '. . . he intends to design a car that will carry the mechanical units without using the classical frame. The hull of a ship is quoted as a possible model. Sgr Lancia also tells us his idea of replacing the rigid front axle by a suspension in which the movements of the wheels would be independent of each other. . . .'

So the Lambda (Tipo 67) took form, powered by a narrow V o.h.c. 4-cylinder unit of 2,120 c.c., high-revving to an unheard of 3,250 r.p.m. The box-like frame was built and the suspension—the first independent front suspension in the world—was completed. Lancia himself drove it on 1 September 1921; *a beautifully sprung, stable, manoeuvrable and safe car* as a contemporary report stated.

After ten years of the Lambda (and the Dilambda) Lancia produced the 1.9-litre Artena, and the Astura, with a 2.6-litre unit, and in 1937—Vincenzo Lancia's last personal design before he died—the small Aprilia, brilliantly packed with technical innovations.

Left Vincenzo Lancia, during his competition days.

OPEN ROAD

The years between the end of World War I and 1930 saw in Europe the appearance of sophisticated and spectacular luxury vehicles, steady technical progress, which gave us most of the advances that we expect to see on modern vehicles, and the rise of the small unspectacular motor car designed to be used by the man who previously had not been able to afford any private transport more costly than the bicycle.

The passing of the *Belle Epoque* of France and other European countries with the war, the relaxing of the stilted conventions of the moneyed Edwardians, the blurring of class demarcation lines, and the wider but thinner spread of car-buying cash, forced motor manufacturers to re-think design, size, quality and cost in the most basic ways.

But even if the first hints of depression had not forced the trend to smaller cheaper cars, the time was ripe for the man-in-the-street to become the man-in-the-car. For two full decades the people's noses had been pressed against the curtained windows of luxury motors; now it was time for the rest of the world to sample the delights of automotive travel.

However, some manufacturers elected to make large and expensive cars immediately after the war.

Napier for instance, produced the ill-fated 40/50 in 1919—and sold precisely 187. The number of manufacturers that survived this early period was considerably smaller than that which succumbed, and even substantial companies like Rolls-Royce, Lanchester and others were occasionally in trouble—although W. O. Bentley chose 1920 to put his first cars on the market, and he cannot be said to have been unsuccessful. . . .

The early vintage car was naturally a product of pre-war research and trial, which was soon to be augmented by rapid developments forced through by the war itself—particularly aero-engine developments in the use of aluminium for pistons, which permitted a much higher engine speed. Standard bodies also began to be seen on the new cars in the showroom soon after the war. Cars had abruptly ceased to be an exotic luxury offered exclusively to the privileged few in chassis form with the choice of trim and coachwork dictated by Her Ladyship's whim. In the brave new world opening up

Below During the 'twenties Bugattis of different types poured out of the Molsheim works; the long-wheelbase Type 22, the 8-cylinder Type 30, the sports and racing Type 35s of various letters, the Type 37, 37A (shown) 38, 40, 41, and others, not necessarily in that order. Yet less than 10,000 Bugatti cars were made.

as the third decade of the twentieth century began, design principles started to take note of the fact that motor transport, having proved itself in war, was about to become very much a part of the daily scene. Motor vehicles were now very much accepted as useful artifacts of commerce, in professional and family life, and were structured accordingly.

In America they were ahead of the game. From the beginning they had designed their cars for work rather than for fun and were beginning to beaver away with post-war production, led of course, by the (now ageing) Model T Ford.

Small-car Europe

And the Tin Lizzie also influenced design thinking on the other side of the Atlantic in no small way. In France, Renault, although keeping some of his older models, had dropped his *Taxi de la Marne*, the famous 9 h.p. of earlier days, and brought out a new 10 h.p., a 4-cylinder car on the lines of (even Renault admits this) the Model T Ford. A couple of years later Renault began making his larger cars—from 20 to 45 h.p.—but was always better known, like his arch-rival André Citroën, for his multitude of smaller vehicles.

Citroën, who had made shells for France during the 1914–18 war, burst upon the automotive scene in 1919 with his Type A, designed by an engineer from the Paris *Ecole des Arts et Métiers*. The 4-cylinder 1,327 c.c. car with a French Treasury rating of 8 h.p. had a maximum speed of about 45 m.p.h. and was at first sold for a modest 8,000 Francs. It appealed to the new public, and in 1921 10,000 were made, a feat largely due to the standardization of Citroën production methods at the new factory at the Quai de Javel. By 1926 Citroën

was making cars in Great Britain, Germany and Italy, mostly in the lower price bracket. Primarily an innovator, André Citroën himself was a master of ingenuity, who dived happily into technical problems, and his enquiring mind led to the pioneering by his company of mass-produced all-steel bodies, rubber-block mounted engines, vacuum servo brakes, the 6-cylinder four-bearing engine, low-pressure tyres and, in 1934, the most significant of all, *traction avant*—front wheel drive.

In Germany, a country with its own unhappy problems, life for the car manufacturer was bedevilled by the diving value of the Mark. Opel, one of the founders of European motor industry which, like Wartburg and its descendants, does not seem to get its share of the credit for its early work, was nevertheless bold enough to adapt to the changing markets of the 'twenties, and was the first German company to use conveyer belt systems, leading directly to its little *Laubrosch* in 1924 (a near-copy of the Citroën 5CV), a 4-cylinder utility, which within four years of production outsold everything else in the country.

In spite of post-war recovery problems, it was the Golden 'Twenties for motoring in Germany. Although there was a 10% purchase tax on cars, a glut of American-made vehicles in the showrooms, and the fact that German industry lagged technically, prices were whittled down steadily in the early 'twenties, introducing great numbers of people to the delights of the open road. On the horizon of 1928, however, loomed the

Below 1922, brink of the age of mobility for the family, who up to now had used the charabanc for leisure travel. The 'Bullnose' Morrises are being produced now, and Herbert Austin is about to offer his first Austin Seven to the British public.

Great Depression. Domestic sales of Opel and other German companies began to drop. Opel became part of General Motors in 1928, two years after Benz and Daimler had decided to find greater strength in amalgamation.

In Italy, indestructible Fiat came out of the war smiling. The Tipo Zero had got mass production into gear in 1913, and now the 501, a tough welded-frame low-price 1½-litre car that all Italy wanted to buy, helped recovery. In 1922, the company produced its 6.8-litre 'Superfiat' against much advice, but this was a mark of faith, a prestige car that in true vintage tradition was constructed superbly and sold only to the rich and discriminating—some 30 models in the first two years.

Superfiat was in fact an attempt to live in the rarified atmosphere of the upper echelons of the automotive world, with that small coterie of manufacturers that were, right through the 'twenties, making some of the most superbly-constructed quality cars that have ever been made. The Bentleys, Hispano-Suizas, Bugattis, Lagondas, Rolls-Royces and Delages were artworks in the finest handcraft tradition, often spiced by the new image of sportive luxury. To compare them with the present-day best would be to injure both—the basic purposes and uses were widely different; but with the sliding scale of judgment that must be used as the years pass, it will be appreciated by anyone who as much as pokes his nose over the high side of a Vauxhall 30/98, or into any of the multiplicity of types that the astonishing Ettore Bugatti built in such sparing numbers, or a Daimler Double-Six, a Lancia Lambda, a period Packard or Stutz or Pierce-Arrow, that here was the zenith of the art of the car-builder, with their silky woodwork, milled aluminium, multiple coats of painstakingly applied paint, torpedo bodies lightly designed for summer and the elegant towny coupé-de-ville styles showing still a little Edwardian convention through their new thrusting lines.

Led by France, the *conduite intérieure*—the saloon— slowly took over from the button-up mica sidescreen windows of the tourer, although until the mid 'twenties they were built comparatively high—not as is often said so that passengers could wear hats but simply because no-one had yet thought of lowering the suspension and headroom (and centre of gravity) in a normal road car. And there were still old ladies around who would remark that one should always be able to *walk into* a proper car without bending. . . .

To some, the vintage years have an expansive aura of motoring leisure about them, and indeed they were grand years for those whose pleasures included racing the *Blue Train* down to Cannes. But for the overwhelming majority, these years were the ones that opened doors to the first modest essays into the motoring world; to the Saturday spin, the touring holiday in Scotland, the freedom of the open road. Whilst Rolls-Royce brought out their Phantom Twenty and sold about 3,000 of them in four years, Morris was supplying the impecunious with his Bullnoses—and sold 54,000

of them in a single year. And in America, understandably, the figures were beginning to become astronomical, with no less than 3,783,987 cars produced in 1926 alone.

The 'twenties, at least the second half of them, were also beginning to see a new generation of amateur mechanics, people whose burning ambition was to become a motorist, whose pocket was short, and who maintained and repaired whatever they could afford to buy, in their own backyard.

Spooning in a Ford

The call of the open road was loud and clear. Motor advertisements began to change in attitude. Earlier ones had shown the Master getting into his motor car after the hunt; now they depicted the young couple doing a spot of moonlight spooning in their small Ford or Austin.

Herbert Austin, the man who put Britain on British wheels was one of the most colourful and determined

Above Sporting British. The Hon. V. A. Bruce (left) poses with his A.C. after winning the 1926 Monte Carlo Rally. He was the only British competitor.
Below The ubiquitous Tin Lizzie, the Ford Model T, on the open road in the moonlight, performing another useful function.

men in the motor industry. As manager of a sheep-shearing tool works under the Wolseley banner he first made his own experimental cars, caught the financial interest of Frederick Wolseley, put that company on the motoring map, then left to produce his own cars in a derelict printing works in Longbridge, Birmingham.

But if Herbert Austin had made only one model, he would have been sure of his place in history because of the Austin 7, first seen in 1922. The cramped, much-loved product of Austin's desire to equip the public with automotive transport was to be the first proud vehicle of many a Briton. The car's magnificent simplicity, its straightforward sequences of mechanics, proved a boon to the new motoring millions of the decade following World War I and a foundation for many an engineering intellect that was to flower later.

In 1912 W. R. Morris, a garage proprietor in the university town of Oxford, had produced his first light car, the Morris Oxford, and later the larger Cowley, both sporting monobloc engines by White and Poppe. Through the war Morris had imported U.S. 'Continental' engines and when peace was resumed the Cowley was back at £465 for the two-seater, reducing in 1922 to £225, and capturing a market that had been thought the preserve of his competitors.

The 'Bullnose' Cowleys of the early 'twenties housed a 1,550 c.c. engine, had three forward speeds plus reverse and rear-wheel-brakes-only until 1926; and from the humble Morris sprang the livelier M.G. sports car. Cecil Kimber, who was in charge of William Morris' old firm, began experimenting with the Oxford, building a new body, tuning the engine and calling it the M.G. Super Sports. Its lightweight open body and handling ensured popularity, and the M.G. line was born. The later Morris Minor became the M.G.

Above Bentley, the quintessence of 'twenties racing. This 1929 supercharged 4½-litre former team Bentley is seen here at Oulton Park, circulating at considerable speed.

Below The Opel Laubfrosch. This little 4-cylinder 951 c.c. 'Tree-Toad' was the first assembly-line produced German car. Made from 1924 to 1927, Opel sold nearly 40,000.

M-type Midget, tuned to give 65 m.p.h. in 1929. By 1930 the M.G. was ready for racing.

Other marques that captured the interest of many in Britain with more or less restricted funds were the Riley—the smart sports Redwing with a 1½-litre unit was the dream of many a would-be owner—the Rover, in economy guise with a flat-twin 1-litre Eight (sold for as little as £160 in 1925) with lots of glass and a curtained rear window, the two-seater Wolseley 10, a 1¼-litre ohv with a racing version called the 'Moth', the Singer Junior with its 848 ohc engine, the new (in 1923) Triumph 10/20 at £430, and, in a remote, impossible-dream way, the Vauxhall 30/98 then vying with the 4½-litre Bentley for sporting honours.

In the 'twenties middle class fathers learned, carefully and meticulously, to drive the family car (even wealthy dads began to take an interest in driving instead of sitting in luxury leather and letting the chauffeur do the work), grandparents learned to sit in the back and marvel, mum discovered that weekends could be spent away from the cooker and the kids took eagerly to picnic jaunts. Their motor car, be it a third-hand hack bought for a fiver or a brand new Oxford (they knew little about the more exotic machinery—Sunbeams, Lagondas, or the new Aston Martins) was their magic carpet to the new world of the coast or the hills and the pleasant winding road.

And the motorist of the 'twenties certainly had all he needed in the way of an open road. All he had to do was point his car in the desired direction and go, without any significant let or hindrance from other traffic. In the suburbs of large cities car-spotting was one of the hobbies of the young—collecting registration numbers to complete a series. Marque spotting too, was a favourite game—watching a distant car approach and

Above In the late 'twenties Daimler-Benz were making three classic Mercedes models, the Stuttgart, the Mannheim and, in 1928, the six-seater Nürburg, shown here. Produced to appeal to the luxury market, as the advertisement indicates, it housed an 8-cylinder 4·6-litre unit.

Below Modelling in the 'twenties—two heavily draped ladies show the 1925 Austin Seven Tourer.

getting in first with the maker's name. Space and time there was, out of sight of the local bobby, to play roller-skate hockey on suburban roads, and a passing car was merely another occasional hazard.

This decade saw the final disappearance of Edwardian philosophy (cars were either slow and comfortable, or fast, noisy and damned uncomfortable) and saw the birth of the modern light car (in place of the abominable cycle-car). And it saw concurrently the development of the no-expense-spared luxury vehicle in which the peak of craftsmanship and individuality, the like of which has rarely been matched, marked them down as later collectors' jewels. This decade saw American cars change from the brutish to the sophisticated, and it saw Cadillac give the synchro-mesh to the automotive world. In this decade Weyman developed the flexible wood-frame saloon body, covered in fabric to cut the cost of making a closed car, thus helping to swing the trend from tourers to closed models. In the 'twenties four-wheeled brakes became universal, low-pressure tyres were introduced and Ford and General Motors blossomed into massive-scale production. These years

saw the birth of the universal motoring age, when the car became the first purchase after the house; they saw the end of the Model T, the beginning of the flood of small continental cars, the passing of a thousand motor manufacturers, the opening of the first roadside filling station, the building of the first by-passes, the establishing of roadhouse restaurants.

And finally, at the end of the 'twenties, we saw the beginning of the end of the open road, when the ever-increasing numbers of Clynos, Beans, Swifts, Trojans, Austins, Stars, Morrises and Calthorpes slowly but inexorably began to over-occupy the space provided for them and started the long sad process of clogging the open road to those very places the car had been designed to take people to see and enjoy. . . .

Above Morris Minor 1928, in idyllic rural setting; 847 c.c. and o.h.c. for £125.

Top right Citroën's 5CV, 1922. In various forms (including the famous cloverleaf three-seater) this little car, often said to be neither a good goer or a good stopper, was nevertheless almost indestructible, and immensely popular. It was made until 1925, and some may still be seen on the roads of France.

BIG FAKE

Elderly gentlemen raised their hats and huffed, 'They don't make them like that any more!' when they saw it pass by. Traffic smilingly made way for it on main roads. Veteran car fans looked puzzled—and looked again in a vain endeavour to date the thing. It looked as though it was born about 1919; its racy bonnet line and boat-tail put it in the sporting class, and its heavy brass lamps and levers indicated a rather vulgar Edwardian heritage.

In fact it was made in 1968 by car-builder Alan Mann of Surrey, England, housed a V6 Ford engine, had automatic gears, a top speed of 100 m.p.h.—and drove like a crazy fire-engine. The car was made for the Film Chitty-Chitty-Bang-Bang and (very approximately) based on Count Zborowski's 1920 car of the same name.

But this big fake delighted a lot of children for several years—and it fooled some of the people some of the time. . . .

Above The big coppery pipes were, sadly, mere decoration. They conveyed no exhaust gases and produced no power roar.

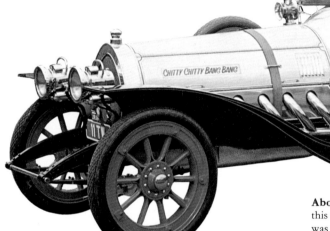

Above Based—very sketchily—on Count Zborowski's 1920 car, this Chitty-Chitty-Bang-Bang was beautiful, but false. However, it was the star of a popular film and is remembered by thousands of children better than the original.

Bottom Too Edwardian to be true? The profusion of levers and dials and brasswork and boat-deck was typical of the day.

VETERAN VIEW

Most of the roads were loose gravel, smooth enough after the rutted tracks of previous centuries, and safer. In the last days of Queen Victoria, Britain's rural roads were peaceful, green, their silence broken only by a clopping carter's horse and the clatter of a wood pigeon's wings as the sound flushed him out. Now and again a faint put-put-put could be heard and the children would run to the front gate to see the passing horseless carriage or motored bicycle rattle past the house.

In the quiet provincial spa town of Bath the horse-drawn carriage was ubiquitous, and travel was still slow and leisured; for long distances there was always the train. This was the world of young Harold Davis, born in 1891, the year of the first Panhard–Levassor, and now 83 years old—one of the few present-day drivers who can recall early motoring days in England.

'Dust,' says veteran Harold Davis, 'that was the great frustrating factor of those days. Although there were few enough of us on the roads, if you travelled in an urban area behind another vehicle—or in a following wind—you could be choked with the stuff. No wonder the residents complained. Right up into the 'twenties one could drive over country roads leaving a solid mile of dust-cloud behind.'

Eighty years ago Londoners still considered the horseless carriage a device of the devil, and even animals took an instinctive dislike to it. When a small De Dion crossed one of London's bridges in 1899 it was unlucky enough to meet a troop of cavalry—and scattered them faster than if they had sighted a party of Boers.

In the provinces of Britain motor cars appeared on the scene a little later—and brought universal dislike for the motorist with them. And who could blame the country folk—the earliest cars in Britain were smokey, noisy, unpredictable and often downright uncontrollable. And besides, they frightened people. . . .

'Up until 1906 cars were a rare sight outside London,' said Harold Davis. 'But I saw my first car—it was probably a Peugeot—when I lived in Bath, when my cousin drove one along the Wells Road into the city of Bath in the spring of 1896.' That was in the last year of the regulation requiring a footman to precede the motor vehicle. 'I actually remember a solemn bowler-hatted pedestrian marching in front of a passenger car in Bath at that time, just before the implementation of the 1896 Act,' said Mr. Davis.

Like most mechanically-orientated young men of the day Harold Davis began on motor cycles—the push-and-jump-on clutchless type—in this case a Bradbury, which he drove regularly from London to Worthing.

'We soon got to know all the blacksmiths on the route,' he says, 'as they were the only points where we

Above Harold Norman Davis. Over 65 years since his first drive—in an early Mercedes—and still a highly competent driver.

could buy petrol and get some sort of repair work done.'

In 1908, young Harold Davis had his first four-wheel drive—he took one of the first Mercedes cars on a round-the-block trip. 'Since it was an old car even then,' he says, 'it was probably an early Simplex model.' Earlier still, back in 1902, he had moved with his family to Covent Garden in London. 'We drove in an open cab from Paddington station,' he says, 'and didn't see a single motor vehicle. I know, because as an 11-year-old motoring enthusiast I was keenly looking out for one!'

By 1909, Harold Davis was an accomplished motor cyclist. Long solitary journeys to the south coast were punctuated by adventures typical of pioneer days. 'Like running out of carbide one evening while I was riding my $\frac{3}{4}$ h.p. N.S.U.' he relates, 'The headlamp began to fail, and although I had a little reserve carbide, I could find no water (the two mixed together produced a gas which one ignited to produce a very reasonable light). So I tipped the remaining carbide into the container and produced the water in nature's own way. Not quite the way to behave on the road today!'

'It couldn't have been such a good beam that night, though,' said Harold Davis, 'for at the village of Findon just a few miles north of Worthing I forked right—straight into a horse-pond—and then had to dive under the water to retrieve the bike. When I looked in at the village pub for a warming drink, I was met with gales of laughter. It seemed that dunked motor cyclists were a regular entertainment there.'

Harold Davis has driven regularly since he was 18 years old; his first motor cycles, a Lanchester, his father's early Studebaker, a bull-nosed Morris, a twin-cylinder Rover (1921 vintage) and countless others, culminating with his present 3.5-litre Rover.

His recollections of the roads in Britain half-a-century-and-more ago are evocative of a more dignified age—of perhaps a 1901 voiturette owned by his grandfather, or a spindly 10 h.p. Gladiator, the first 6-cylinder Napiers, Straker-Squire buses with their solid tyres side-slipping on wood-block London roads, of the high-ride handle-barred Indian motor-cycle he rode to Clacton from London in 90 minutes half-a-century ago, of quiet suburban London in the 'twenties—and of the only

Above A 4½ h.p. single cylinder de Dion engined Mayfair voiturette of 1901. At the wheel, Henry Davis, Mr. Harold Davis' grand-father.

time he has been booked by the police. He was accused of *exceeding the speed limit in a Royal Park*, to wit, Regents Park, in the days when the limit was 20 m.p.h. And that time he admits he was asking for trouble. Says Harold: 'There was no other traffic about and I had my feet on the handlebars, and was leaning back enjoying the fresh air. I sailed through a concealed trap and was booked on the spot. Why they ignored the highly gymnastic way I was conducting the vehicle I'll never know!'

That was, of course, a few years back. . . .

ACKNOWLEDGMENTS

With the exception of illustrations on the following pages, all colour and black and white photographs come from Peter Roberts' Collection. *Autocar*: pp. 24–5, below p. 49 *H. N. Davis*: above p. 127, above p. 128 *Goodyear*: below p. 60 *National Motor Museum*: top right p. 27, right pp. 36–37, top right p. 53, right p. 99.

In addition, the author and publishers are most grateful to the following organizations for help in research and for providing (often very rare) illustrations for this book:

Alfa Romeo, American Motors Corporation, Automobile Association. B.L.M.C., B.P., Chrysler U.K. & International, Citroën, Daimler-Benz, Fiat, Ford Motor Company, General Motors, Goodyear, Lancia, Mercedes-Benz G.B., Motor Vehicle Manufacturers Association U.S.A., Adam Opel A.G., Automobiles Peugeot, *Punch*, Renault, Rolls-Royce, Skoda, Vauxhall.